Advance Praise for *Mission in Captivity*

"This powerful personal memoir represents more than one individual's struggle for survival; It serves as a profound moral compass for a world grappling with the resurgence of an age-old blind, hatred. Shoshan's courageous journey speaks to the very foundations of human resilience and to our eternal hope for a shared future defined by life and dignity."

—Isaac Herzog, President of the State of Israel

"A searing reminder of the hell the hostages had to endure. While serving as the US Special Envoy to Monitor and Combat Antisemitism, I had the privilege of working with Dr. Haran after she and part of her family were released, as she fought like a lioness for the freedom of her son-in-law and the other hostages. Now she comes to tell that story. It is a gripping read."

—Ambassador Deborah Lipstadt

"Among so many riveting and heartbreaking accounts of the October 7, 2023, massacre and kidnapping by Hamas, Dr. Shoshan Haran's testimony is deeply spellbinding and moving. A resident of Kibbutz Be'eri who dedicated her life to agricultural advancements that brought prosperity and health to the disadvantaged in Africa, her kindness and commitment were repaid with fifty days in captivity, the murder of her beloved husband, the destruction of her home, and the suffering of so many whom she loved and admired.

Dr. Haran emerged from this catastrophe determined to go on, to continue her mission, and to try to make sense of a world gone mad. Needless to say, it is a daunting task but one that she handles with sensitivity and brilliance.

Mission in Captivity is an essential component of the testimonies that are required to understanding and moving forward in the wake of the greatest calamity to befall the Jewish People since the Holocaust. It is a must read."

—David Friedman, Former United States Ambassador to Israel

"Nearly three years after October 7, the most barbaric attack on the Jews since the Holocaust, Dr. Shoshan Haran recounts the suffering she and her family experienced, starting with the slaughter in her home of Kibbutz Be'eri to months of captivity in Gaza. *Mission in Captivity* is essential reading so that people do not forget the atrocities of that day and the months after for the hostages. A humanitarian, scientist and lifelong peace seeker, Dr. Haran's writing offers a rare burst of humanity and light amid depths of darkness and her voice is deeply needed today."

—Bernard-Henri Lévy

"*Mission in Captivity* is a harrowing, deeply human account of spirit and survival in the face of terror. Dr.

Shoshan Haran's story shines a light on the courage of the hostages, the resilience of their families, and the long path to healing after the horrors Hamas carried out on October 7. This is a story that everyone should read—and remember."

—Ted Deutch, CEO of AJC

MISSION IN CAPTIVITY

ONE WOMAN'S STRUGGLE TO SURVIVE AND SAVE HER FAMILY IN GAZA

DR. SHOSHAN HARAN

HEBREW EDITION EDITED BY AVIV HAVRON
TRANSLATED FROM THE ORIGINAL HEBREW BY EYLON LEVY

WS
WICKED SON

A WICKED SON BOOK
An Imprint of Post Hill Press
ISBN: 979-8-89565-774-4
ISBN (eBook): 979-8-89565-775-1

Mission in Captivity:
One Woman's Struggle to Survive and Save Her Family in Gaza

Cover Design by Conroy Accord

This is a work of nonfiction. All people, locations, events, and situations are portrayed to the best of the author's memory.

Post Hill Press
New York • Nashville
wickedsonbooks.com
posthillpress.com

Published in the United States of America
1 2 3 4 5 6 7 8 9 10

"I never considered myself important enough to feel tempted to tell others the story of my life. Much had to happen, far more in the shape of terrible events, disasters and trials than any other single generation has known, before I found the courage to embark on a book in which I feature as the main or, more accurately, the central character.... I have been a defenceless, helpless witness of the unimaginable relapse of mankind into what was believed to be a long-forgotten barbarism, with its deliberate programme of inhuman dogma."

—*The World of Yesterday*, Stefan Zweig[1]

---

1 Zweig, S. (2009). *The World of Yesterday* (A. Bell, Trans.). Pushkin Press. (Original work published 1942). All subsequent quotations from Stefan Zweig are from *The World of Yesterday*, translated by Anthea Bell (Pushkin Press, 2009).

Dedicated to Avshal, the love of my life

TABLE OF CONTENTS

PART 3: RESOLVE

PREFACE

BOOKS ARE MY REFUGE. I have always treasured them as a window into other souls, other places, other periods, other thoughts. Into whole worlds. Since I was a girl, I have always been a bookworm. Now, they are also a lifeline. To save myself from thinking, to find a refuge from the emptiness that threatens to drag me into the abyss, I read and read and read.

I am currently reading Stefan Zweig's *The World of Yesterday* for the second time. Amazed at its prescience, at how it captures what we went through and are still going through. And the prose is so thought-provoking and sublime, especially when he describes the erosion of morality:

> "For in the midst of his military and political victories, that was Hitler's most diabolic triumph --- one man succeeded in deadening every idea of what is just and right by the constant attrition of excess. Before this 'New Order' was ushered in, the world would have been horrified if a single human being had been murdered for no reason, and without recourse to the law.... After the annexation of Austria in 1938, our world became inured to inhumanity, injustice and brutality as never before

> in hundreds of years. Once what happened in the unfortunate city of Vienna alone would have been internationally condemned, but in 1938 the conscience of the world kept quite, or murmured just a little before forgetting and forgiving."

Just replace the names and dates, and the words are chillingly relevant.

Today, in Be'eri, in Israel, and around the world—perhaps only in relation to Israelis and Jews?—the word "murder" has become banal. Men were murdered, women were murdered, the elderly were murdered, children were murdered, and most cruelly of all, the youngest victim of the massacre—nine-month-old Mila Cohen—was murdered in her mother's arms.

Murder has gone from being a one-off event that shocks an entire country to a fact of daily life that rolls off the tongue. So bland. So trite. Practically a casual aside. Almost as mundane as walking or eating.

And then there is the word "hostage." Hundreds of hostages. Including toddlers, children, women, men, the elderly. Including us. These words are impossible to swallow. The same for "atrocities." And "burned houses."

Abandoned, betrayed, helpless, defenseless. Pogroms. Conquest. Abuse. Kidnapping. Murder. Rape. And nobody came to shield or save us.

My country, where were you? Our world, where were you?

I am acutely aware of the power and immense importance of books. They tell stories, commit them to a tangible record, save them from erasure. And I understand, this time, it is I who must tell the story to others. I must tell what happened to me. To us. I must share facts, thoughts, feelings, lessons.

I must tell the truth. Because this is what happened.

PART 1
CAPTIVITY

CHAPTER I

THE WORLD OF YESTERDAY

Wednesday, October 4, 2023

AS ALWAYS, I WAKE UP before Avshal and head out for a morning walk through the small gate in the security fence that encircles Kibbutz Be'eri. I turn west. The border with the Gaza Strip is scarcely three miles away, but I feel no fear. We have been promised that the Israel Defense Forces (IDF), camped out in military bases between us and the border, are keeping us safe.

I start along the narrow road that winds between fields to the north, freshly plowed for potato season, and the mango and avocado groves to the south. I love walking in these early hours when the air is still crisp and cool. My head is clear, echoing with the upbeat melody of the Palmach Anthem[2]. It was a song the

---

[2] Gilead, Zerubavel. The Palmach Anthem" (Hymn of the Palmach). Music by David Zehavi, 1941.

pioneers who founded our kibbutz in 1946 sang often, and now it plays in my head like a rhythmic pulse:

Gaze, look, and see:
How great is this day!
A fire burns in my chest
And the plow breaks the soil once more.
Hoe, mattock, spade and pitchfork
Have come together in a storm,
And again we will kindle the earth
With a green flame.

The song's rhythm, optimism, and theme of working the land keep me company like a meditative mantra on my morning walk.

To the right of the road I notice potato seeds scattered over the tilled soil. From the label on the sacks, I recognize the company that developed this variety. And what a funny coincidence: In three days' time, on October 7, I am set to fly to the Netherlands to meet this company's seed producers and discuss cooperation with Fair Planet, the nonprofit I founded to help small farmers in Africa access better seeds and advanced agricultural knowledge.

I reach a fork in the road and take a right toward Nahbir, the spot where my parents, Rina and Abraham Havron founded Kibbutz Be'eri with another twenty-seven enthusiastic young pioneers before the community moved to its current location. Flanking me are dry streambeds, twisting between rounded hillocks covered in fresh greenery that sprang up after the first rains of the season. The road rises and falls; my heartbeat quickens and slows in synchrony.

When I reach Nahbir, I see the old water tower and the security building, a solitary stone structure the kibbutz veterans nicknamed "Mickey Mouse" because the two guard posts on the roof look like the ears of the famous cartoon character. The walls, which survived the Egyptian military offensive during Israel's War of Independence in 1948, are pocked with bullet marks and shell impacts, yet they still stand. Inside, my mother once set up a small museum describing the earliest days of the kibbutz at this spot. To the left of the road, opposite the water tower, there are dugout trenches lined with old sandbags that served as shelter for the kibbutz's members during enemy bombardments in the war of 1948.

The road continues to wind downward, and to the south, a Bedouin shepherd boy leads a flock of sheep. I am always amazed by how a lone shepherd can direct dozens of sheep from one grazing area to another so neatly.

I keep walking along the winding road, and then, spaced at regular intervals, red-and-white observation towers come into view, towering over the high border fence between us and the Gaza Strip. Above them hovers a massive helium balloon, hundreds of feet up in the air, fitted with advanced cameras that observe Gaza around the clock.

The border, sealed with a barrier above and below ground, surveillance systems, sensors, and high-tech equipment, was sold to us, the residents of this border region known as the "Gaza Envelope," as the pinnacle of defensive technology. We were told that all these gizmos would provide real-time intelligence on the movements of Hamas and Palestinian Islamic Jihad, giving the IDF enough time to respond to any attack—if and when one came.

This is the technology and the army that will fail us in three days, when terrorists with thousands of raging civilians in tow breach the fence, invade our communities, murder 1,200 souls, and abduct 231 civilians and 20 soldiers.

I reach a T-junction, near a beautiful spot where we often meet for picnics beneath the shade of eucalyptus trees during anemone season, when the ground is painted a vivid red. I turn back and walk home the same way I came.

We are in the middle of the Jewish festival of Sukkot, a holiday break. The weather is pleasant, and the forecast is calling for a slight drop in temperatures. Avshal, my husband, is planning to go sailing on a yacht he rented with friends after completing his skipper's course last week. The weather in the Mediterranean is perfect today, and for the first time, my Avshal will be the skipper.

I get home and, before Avshal heads out to sea, we plan the tasks we will need to complete before my daughter Adi arrives with her family. They are coming to stay with us for the eve of Simchat Torah at the end of the Sukkot holiday.

Avshal leaves, and I call my little sister, Lilach, who lives with her husband, Evyatar (we call him Tari), about three hundred feet away, in the westernmost house on the kibbutz. I love visiting her place, joining her on the porch, gorging on the juicy red mulberries she picks from the tree she planted with Tari in the yard, and watching the sun set over the jojoba grove just beyond her garden fence.

Lilach, taller and more slender than me, with wavy black hair and bright eyes, almost always dressed in colorful cotton tunics, strolls over with a jar of homemade chocolate chip cookies. Avshal has a sweet tooth for them, and she feels like pampering him. Over a cappuccino, we make plans to meet up and drive to the huge event that Women Wage Peace and Women of the Sun, a Palestinian women's organization, are holding tonight on a beach on the northern Dead Sea.

Vivian Silver, my friend from across the street, is one of the founders of Women Wage Peace and has been a leading activist since its establishment. The women's movement, with over forty-five thousand members from across Israeli society, hopes to end the Israeli–Palestinian conflict, in partnership with Palestinian women's movements, through a respectful and mutually acceptable political accord. Lilach is an active member; I'm less involved. I devote most of my time to Fair Planet in Africa, so I only join their events from time to time.

Vivian, who has fought like a lioness for a political resolution to the conflict with the Palestinians, said at one of the movement's rallies in 2018:

> Enough! We can't go on without a political horizon. We can't accept operations and acts of war that bring only death, destruction and pain, and inflict mental and physical harm, as a daily occurrence.... We call on the Prime Minister, the Defense Minister and the Cabinet to find the necessary courage to promote political alternatives, which will bring us peace and security.... We call on our sisters in Gaza: join us and call on your leaders, enough! Terror benefits no one. You, too, deserve peace and security.[3]

---

3 WWP Editor, "Vivan Silver, Peace Activist Confirmed Killed—Announcement and Media Coverage," Women Wage Peace, November 14, 2023, https://www.womenwagepeace.org.il/en/vivian-silver-peace/.

Vivian helped me when I founded Fair Planet, sharing advice, connecting me to international development contacts, and guiding me through how to focus our activities in Africa.

Lilach and I get on our bicycles and pedal together, passing the kindergartens, climbing the path that cuts across the kibbutz's central lawn, encircled by tall, broad-canopied ficus trees, and finally, breathless, parking our bikes in the plaza surrounding the communal dining hall.

We sit down for lunch with Tari and Paul, his caregiver, while the bustle of children and adults and the clatter of dishes fills the air around us. Everything radiates the carefree routine of a vibrant, life-affirming community.

After lunch, we take a transit van from the kibbutz's shared carpool and pick up six more women who have signed up for the event.

During the drive, I look at the invitation and see that they are planning a rally to resemble a "negotiating table," preceded by an installation called "Pieces of Peace." I ask Lilach what that means, and she explains: The idea is to create a patchwork quilt from a million pieces of fabric, from all over Israel and the world. Jewish and Arab women, and women of all faiths, will each receive a fourteen-by-fourteen-inch square to embroider or paint with a message of peace. The resulting quilt will serve as a powerful joint call for peace.

On the way, I doze off, as I always do on long drives, and wake up near Jerusalem as the road twists and descends toward the Dead Sea. We get out and join a march of thousands of women (and a few men) all dressed in white—that's the dress code—and march along the desert road toward the event.

After the gathering, speakers from both women's organizations take the stage, brimming with optimism about the power of women to lead a nonviolent resolution of the conflict and prevent suffering on both sides. The event ends with singers on stage, so full of hope for a better future, and we return home.

At home, Avshal, tanned from sailing (as always, he couldn't be bothered to wear a hat against the sun), gushes about his first time as skipper and about how much he enjoyed the freedom and his independence at the helm. A friend who took some pictures during the excursion sends me a photo two days later. There is Avshal, gripping the wheel with two steady hands, his body upright, sunglasses on his smiling face, his gaze fixed straight ahead, his stance proud and confident. The sea and the future lie at his feet.

Or so it seems.

Thursday, October 5, 2023

The Simchat Torah holiday is fast approaching, and with it all our preparing, shopping, and cooking. Friday nights and holiday meals have always been the highlights of our family life in Be'eri. We start preparing for the Shabbat meal on Thursday evening, and Avshal and I have a set division of tasks. He makes a luscious, spicy *matbucha* dip from tomatoes and hot peppers cooked for hours over a low flame. He roasts eggplants to serve up an eggplant and tahini salad that has all of us licking our lips. On Friday mornings, he sets a huge pot on the gas stove, filled with a medley of fresh vegetables, roots, and herbs, and cooks a clear soup—strictly vegetarian for the many vegetarians in our family.

As the soup comes to a boil, building up the bold flavors that will outshine even traditional chicken soup, Avshal sets up a bourguignon-style meat stew for the carnivores among us, then heads out with friends for a vigorous bike ride through the fields of Be'eri. When he returns, he hurries back out to buy a pair of fragrant challah loaves from a bakery in the nearest town.

Meanwhile, I make a quiche or a tofu-and-vegetable curry for the vegetarians, a fresh lettuce salad with a mustard-honey-lemon dressing, and a cake for dessert. Avshal often teases me that even though he spends hours cooking, working, shopping, and serving, the praise for the vegetarian dishes is always louder than the compliments for his own. Which, of course, isn't true.

For the eve of Simchat Torah, which this year falls on Friday, October 6, we invite Adi and Tal, along with our little grandchildren, Naveh and Yula. Adi and Tal used to live in Be'eri, and their children were born here, but they left in 2020. The security situation was too brittle, and the threat of rocket fire from Gaza, a constant menace for over twenty years, was ever-present. The young family made their new home in the Lower Galilee, in northern Israel.

We share a close and warm bond, and we are enamored with our grandkids. Naveh is our eldest grandchild, the one who granted us that coveted status of grandma and grandpa. The lucky ones who get to spoil the kids and enjoy quality time with them without the daily grind of caring for their upbringing.

Avshal and Naveh are especially close. As soon as Naveh shows up, they spend hours together, playing soccer on the lawn, visiting the kibbutz petting zoo, and going on outings together. Yula is still tiny and clings closely to her parents, although I do manage to tempt her into drawing, building things, and playing cards and memory games with me.

I climb the iron stairs to the guest unit we have built on the floor above us, my arms laden with fresh towels and sheets. The steps are painted a pale sky blue, and a grapevine curls around the railing, snaking up from our yard. As I climb, I notice the shutters on the safe-room window are cloaked in dust, and I think to myself: *It's probably time to clean those too.*

Adi, Tal, and the children arrive late at night. They like to make the long drive down from the north in the late hours, when the children can sleep in the car.

Friday, October 6, 2023

Our morning starts relatively late. Adi, Tal, and the children are tired from the late-night drive, and it is still the Sukkot holiday break.

When I hear the pitter-patter of Naveh's feet coming down the stairs, I start making him a hot chocolate. I dissolve cacao powder and sugar in boiling water, then top it with mountains of milk foam, steamed with our coffee machine's frothing wand. In my grandson's world, "Grandma's Real Be'eri Hot Chocolate" is a brand unto itself. Yula joins us a little later, still in pajamas, her blond curls tousled. She asks for and receives her traditional hot chocolate too.

Soon after we finish cooking, Avshal takes Naveh out for a bike ride. Naveh sits in the small seat mounted on the handlebars, Avshal's arms wrapped around him, and they set sail along the winding paths between the fields and orchards, up hills and down through the dry riverbeds, westward, toward the border with Gaza. As they roll along, Avshal takes a selfie of them enjoying themselves, Naveh's hair fluttering in the wind, Avshal's face peeking out behind him. Happy. That is the last photo we have of Avshal.

Meanwhile, Yula is playing with Adi in the play corner at home, Tal is still upstairs in the guest unit, and I'm getting ready to fly to the Netherlands after Shabbat, together with Alon Haberfeld, my partner in establishing Fair Planet.

I came up with the idea for Fair Planet during a vacation in India with Avshal and our two daughters, Adi and Shaked. By then, I already had more than a decade of experience working for international seed companies that specialize in breeding high-quality seed varieties for farmers around the world.

For years, back when I worked in Be'eri's field crops team, I knew that seeds were the foundation of global food production, the source of almost everything we eat. But only in India did I understand that the high-quality seeds we use to grow food in the developed world were inaccessible to farmers in developing, hunger-stricken countries. They have to use inferior local seeds instead, and the result is meager yields, deficient nutrition, extreme poverty, and a day-to-day struggle for subsistence.

I felt I had to do something to connect the poorest farmers in the world to the best seeds in the world. I knew for certain that if they could plant quality seeds, their yields would rise, their income would grow, and their lives would improve. But the idea felt big and frightening. Who was I, and what power did I have to bring about such change? But then again, I had a sturdy kibbutz upbringing. And in our way of life as a cooperative, the most important value is equality—and, above all, equality of opportunity.

I began listing the personal and professional risks to myself if I stepped out of my comfort zone, if I left my interesting, well-paying employment with international firms in the field of seed development and breeding.

On the one hand, I feared that if I dropped everything for such an ambitious new mission, people would consider the move quixotic or, worse, megalomaniacal. On the other hand, even if

I gave up a coveted position in the seed industry, my family and I faced no threat to our livelihoods. Be'eri is still a collectivist kibbutz, whose members' income is pooled equally among everyone. I also knew that the idea of helping poor farmers increase their income was fully aligned with the egalitarian values of kibbutz life, and I presumed the initiative would win the respect and support of my community.

Moreover, because I knew the people in the seed industry well and knew how deeply they were tied to farmers in the field, I believed they would love the idea too.

The risks seemed minor compared to the vast opportunities of instigating such meaningful change. I decided to go for it. The first step was to try to build a win-win model, one that would be economically beneficial for both poor farmers and seed companies. That was the only chance for real change. It was time to translate ideas into action. In 2012, I left my job in the seed industry and founded Fair Planet, a nonprofit that would help small farmers escape the cycle of hunger and poverty through access to quality vegetable seeds and agricultural know-how. Together with Alon, a longtime colleague who immediately joined my mission, we decided to focus first on Africa, home to the world's most severe hunger hotspots.

The next step was to create partnerships with seed companies, to make the varieties suitable for African climate conditions available to farmers there. We took those seeds to field trials in villages in Ethiopia, our first destination, and identified the optimal varieties for local growing methods and market demands. Later, we recruited professionals and volunteers to train farmers in how to use the seeds properly and achieve robust high-quality yields. Meanwhile, we trained local development agents, who in turn would expand the circles of training. In this way, we put into practice the aphorism that it is better to give a hungry person a rod than a fish—only in our case, it was seeds and knowledge rather than vegetables.

On this upcoming trip, on the Saturday night after Simchat Torah, October 7, Alon and I are set to meet with Dutch seed companies to report the results of a Hebrew University study on the impact of our joint project in Ethiopia.

The findings are exhilarating. Almost all the farmers reported a significant improvement in yields, an increase in sales, and marked rise in annual income. The researchers also found that the farmers were able to use their extra income to improve their own families' nutrition and send their children to school, instead of keeping them at home to help in the fields as before. I am sure that our colleagues in the Netherlands will also be delighted to hear that more than one hundred thousand farmers have already shifted to quality seeds, producing enough fresh vegetables each growing season to feed around eight million people. Another purpose of our meetings in the Netherlands is to discuss advancing further projects in Ethiopia, and even expanding our work into Tanzania and Rwanda.

I pack a carry-on suitcase, organize my handbag, and tuck some new training booklets we prepared for the local farmers into my laptop bag. We have made a mighty effort to develop guidance based on the methods at their disposal, like ox-plowing and furrow irrigation. Our crowning achievement was the development of a method for precise fertilization using drinking bottle caps, basic items available in every African country. We were especially proud of the illustrations demonstrating each step of the growing process, so that even illiterate farmers could follow the instructions.

In the afternoon, the children make decorations for the sukkah we had built on our lawn a week earlier, ahead of Sukkot. Avshal's sister, Sharon, calls to say she will come to visit us with her daughter Noam. Before we head out for the communal holiday meal, we also invite Avshal's mother, Ruth, who moved to Be'eri about three years earlier. Lilach and Tari join as well, and we all sit together around a long table in the large sukkah next to the kibbutz dining hall.

When the meal ends, Lilach and Tari take their leave, and we return home to gather in our own sukkah, adorned with colorful paper chains and our grandchildren's drawings. The table is illuminated with a string of colorful bulbs, glowing against some traditional honey cakes and bowls piled high with my famously crumbly, yummy tahini cookies, baked just as my grandchildren asked. Night falls and turns cool. We all get ready for bed.

CHAPTER II
OCTOBER 7

Saturday, Simchat Torah

I WAKE EARLY TO BIRDSONG fluttering through the branches of the trees around our yard. Early morning is my favorite time of the day. The air is crisp and clean, the house is quiet, and only Avshal's breathing fills our bedroom.

From the day we met, back when we were both young students at the Hebrew University, we knew: I am a morning bird, and he is a night owl. When the kids were born, we used to joke that between us, we had most of the hours of the day pretty much under control.

Our holiday guests are still asleep. Adi, Tal, Naveh, and Yahel are on the floor above us; Sharon and Noam are in the guest room on the ground floor. The smell of cholent spreads through the house, slowly brewing toward our Shabbat lunch. I slip out of the bedroom quietly, still in my pajamas, to add liquid to the stew so it won't burn. Through the large windows looking out onto the yard, I see the sukkah and the dining table, now covered in leaves shaken loose from the roof by the wind, the neighbors' dog darting across our lawn, and the soccer shoes Naveh forgot outside yesterday after his game with Avshal.

I start making hot chocolate for Naveh, always an early-riser, like me.

06:29.

Suddenly, the emergency sirens wail: *Tzeva Adom, Tzeva Adom!* Red Alert! Immediate rocket fire from Gaza. We have only fifteen seconds to get into the safe room. I run back into the bedroom to wake Avshal and see he's already up. On his phone, the Red Alert app is reporting simultaneous attacks across whole swathes of Israel. I used to tease him, *Why do you need to know what's happening with sirens all over the country? Are the sirens in Be'eri not enough?*

But Avshal was right. From the app, he understands immediately: This time, it's something completely different. He races upstairs and urges Adi, Tal, and the kids to come down right away and get into the safe room. They tumble down the stairs, bleary-eyed, Naveh in a red Hapoel Be'er Sheva soccer shirt with his name stitched on and matching shorts, and little Yula in a sweet unicorn top and pink leggings.

We still think this is "just" a rocket fire alert, the kind we have known for the last twenty years. Since Israel withdrew from the Gaza Strip in 2005 and Hamas seized power in a violent coup two years later, Be'eri and neighboring communities have been the targets of sporadic and unpredictable rocket fire. Sadly, running for shelter is part of our daily lives. We always used to say our region is 98 percent paradise and 2 percent hell. Visitors from all over the country come in quieter times to enjoy the beauty, especially in anemone season, when winter paints the open fields a brilliant red. Ironically, that season is branded

Darom Adom, "Red South," which sounds a lot like *Tzeva Adom*: Red Alert.

We are well drilled for emergencies. We must always stay within fifteen seconds of a safe room, and when the siren blares, we rush inside and seal the heavy door and window, both made of steel, until we hear the whistle of an Iron Dome interceptor, in the best case, or the explosion of impact, in the worst. Only then are we allowed to go back to whatever we were doing.

But nobody ever prepared these safe rooms—or us—for a scenario in which terrorists breached the kibbutz itself. Our steel door has no internal lock. Some of our neighbors in Be'eri had even removed the secure steel doors and installed decorative ones instead. But only a few had taken the initiative of installing lock mechanisms so they can seal safe rooms from the inside.

After about ten minutes in the safe room, with no more sirens, we all come out. Barefoot, still wearing pajamas, and with a sheer, colorful shawl I inherited from my mother over my shoulders, I go back to making hot chocolate, this time for all three children.

And then a chilling message flashes in the kibbutz WhatsApp group:

Suspected terrorist infiltration into the kibbutz. Enter the safe room immediately and close the security door.

We obey at once, terrified. Avshal stays outside the safe room, clutching a kitchen knife, peering through the windows to try to understand what is happening outside. To protect us. To protect his family.

A few minutes later, another message:

Terrorist infiltration in Be'eri. Stay in the safe room until further notice.

Pure horror.

I can't believe this is really happening.

There are seven of us crammed into this tiny safe room: Adi, Tal, Naveh, Yahel (whom we fondly call Yula), Sharon, Noam, and me. I close the two steel shutters on windows and anchor them to the windowsill. Suddenly the phone rings. It's my son, Yuval, who has gone for weekend trip in the desert with his girlfriend, Anna-Lee.

"We're all in the safe room," I answer in a whisper. "We're OK."

We hear gunfire nearby. Be'eri's security squad, civilian volunteers tasked with holding off attackers until the army arrives, must be trying to repel the terrorists. For years, our working assumption has been that the IDF, which held a drill simulating a terrorist infiltration in the kibbutz only two months ago, will arrive within twenty to thirty minutes of an attack. Our task is to hold out in our safe rooms and follow the safety instructions.

But then a short while later, we hear shouting. In Arabic only. My brain refuses to take it in. *This cannot be real.* Nobody is shouting back in Hebrew.

The gunfire creeps closer. Grenade explosions too.

We are in the safe room, frozen. Completely helpless. Perfectly silent.

It doesn't feel like this is actually happening to me. I don't feel present. Overwhelmed with fear. *What will happen to us? To the kids? The grandkids?*

Tal braces the safe-room door handle with a heavy wooden plank we use to extend our massive dining table when the full family gathers for meals. Adi and Yula squeeze under the double guest bed together with Sharon and Noam. Naveh stands in the corner behind Tal, thinking there is no more room under the bed. Adi keeps shouting at him to wriggle under, and he manages to squeeze next to Yula. I lie on the floor between the bed and the desk, trying to alert Be'eri's security coordinator and the emergency squad about what I am hearing.

We become increasingly distressed. Flashbacks from Holocaust literature flood my mind. Consumed with overwhelming dread about what is coming.

My phone battery—my phone is the only one that still has reception in the safe room—is draining quickly. Tal remembers there's a flimsy little charger in the desk drawer. I pull it out and plug in my phone. It manages to hold the battery at two percent. That is our only link to the world.

An hour and a half into this horror, Tal texts Avshal from my phone: "Get into the safe room now. You won't stop them with a knife." Avshal concedes. He joins Tal at the door handle, holding the heavy plank firmly in place to prevent the terrorists from opening the steel door from outside.

We are completely silent. Terrified. In disbelief about what is happening. The children are frozen still. My phone keeps filling with messages on the kibbutz's own communal app, Mekomi. "Where is the army?!" But no one shows up. The IDF is meant to belong to us all. It is meant to be a *people's* army, in the fullest sense. It is an army we have all served in at some point in our lives: I was in the Paratroopers, Avshal in the Armored Corps. We have friends who are senior career officers, and many others whose children are in uniform or reserves.

Where is our *army?*

They always promised us we were protected. That despite living so close to Gaza, we were guarded every hour of every day, all year round. There are military bases near Kibbutz Be'eri. Between us and the Gaza Strip, along the border line, is a fence about twenty feet high, sitting above an underground barrier against attack tunnels. This was sold to us as the most sophisticated border security in the world, complete with observation posts, a hovering balloon watching everything inside Gaza, and regular patrols of armed vehicles.

Only two years earlier, on December 7, 2021, the Defense Minister at the time, Benny Gantz, declared: "This barrier, a creative, technological project of the first order, denies Hamas one of the capabilities that it tried to develop and puts a wall of iron, sensors and concrete between it and the residents of the south."

And we believed it.

The community WhatsApp group floods with more and more panicked messages from friends and neighbors who can hear terrorists storming their homes. Constant updates, but no response. Their desperate calls remain unanswered.

Nerve-racking hours pass by. I keep texting with Lilach. I cannot quote our correspondence because the terrorists will soon steal my phone, leaving me without a record. In time, I learn that she manages to contact our brother Aviv, who is in Bhutan on a work trip. "Hearing reports Shaldag special forces are here," she texts him. "We can hear shouting and gunfire near us."

She also texts Inbal Alon, her closest friend and next-door neighbor.

"Sounds like there someone outside," Inbal writes at 07:22.

"In our yard, under the olive trees," Lilach answers in the same minute.

A minute later: "We heard shouting in Arabic."

Inbal, 07:43: "What's happening?"

Lilach, 07:44: "Sounds like they moved away from us."

Inbal, 08:58: "How are you?"

Lilach, 08:59: "In the safe room, waiting for it to end."

Inbal, 09:24: "What's happening??"

Lilach, 09:26: "Scared."

Inbal, 09:32: "What does the silence mean?"

Lilach, 09:36: "No idea."

And then—the conversation runs cold.

Meanwhile, in our own safe room, I receive a WhatsApp message from a Dutch friend, Orlando De Ponti, asking if I am OK. From faraway Holland, he knows what is happening in Be'eri even before our own army.

Avshal's brother Ronen texts from Australia, asking how he can help. I tell him his sister Sharon and her daughter Noam are with us. There is gunfire close by.

There are eight of us now in the safe room. Totally helpless. Totally silent. The gunfire doesn't stop. Grenades are exploding in the neighborhood. We hear the attackers moving closer. Crippling fear. I hear the terrorists entering our house. Shouting in Arabic. Glass shattering. Gunfire. Then silence. Maybe they have moved on.

Hope.

It is an illusion, as I will learn later. At that exact moment, the terrorists break into the house next door, murder my neighbor and friend Orit Svirsky, and abduct her son, Itay. More gunfire. More broken glass.

Then they enter our home, for real this time. Adi and the children are wedged under the bed. Little Yula bursts into tears. Adi tries to calm her in a whisper, wrapping her in a protective embrace.

The sound of gunfire and carnage draws closer, and then the terrorists shout at us through the safe room door: *"Iftah! Iftah! Iftah!"*

Open! Open! Open!

We don't answer.

Suddenly, we hear an almighty explosion. Metal fragments that I guess must be bullets fly inside from the direction of the heavy steel door. As if in slow motion, I see one of them spinning through the air, about eight inches above my head.

"Get your head down, now!" Avshal shouts at me.

On my phone I type: "They're here." I add our address: "Zeitim 508/2." Maybe that will make someone come to rescue us.

No one does.

Silence again. The terrorists fail to break the safe room door. Later, we learn that the explosion jammed the handle and locked the mechanism in place.

A few more minutes of hope. In shock and silence. Then we hear the scraping of heavy machinery through the closed safe room window. We are still trapped in the feeling: *This isn't happening. It can't be.* We can't fathom how we have been abandoned—again and again and again.

Naveh asks Tal, "Daddy, are we going to die now?"

And Tal, who values trust with his children above all and is always totally open with them about everything, cannot bear for the last thing he might say to Naveh to be a lie. So he answers, "I don't know."

10:25.

Almost four hours of this frenzied nightmare.

Avshal texts our son Yuval: *Yuvi, we're in big trouble. Let's hope we get out of this. We love you.*

Yuval asks if terrorists are inside the house.

Avshal manages a brief answer: *We're in the safe room.*

Then the connection runs cold.

10:30.

The safe room's steel window panels begin to bend. The terrorists have brought a bulldozer into the kibbutz. They have already ripped off the iron staircase leading to the second floor, and now they slam the bucket into the thick concrete wall. Avshal lets go of the door handle and vaults over me toward the window.

The bulldozer's bucket manages to warp the window frame, creating a narrow crack between it and the concrete. Through the crack, Avshal sees the terrorist in the driver's seat reversing. Avshal shuts the steel panel again and tries to drive the pin back into the hole in the sill, to keep it shut.

The fear of what will happen if we surrender is paralyzing. Ever since IDF soldier Gilad Shalit was abducted into Gaza in 2006 and returned five years later in a deal that released more than one thousand Palestinian terrorists from prison, we have known that Hamas has been plotting to kidnap Israelis again.

I start imagining the most horrific scenarios of what will happen to us if we give in. We could be abducted into Gaza Strip, murdered, raped, abused, held hostage for who knows how long. The dread becomes a sinking realization.

The bulldozer strikes again, twists the window frame, and forces the crack wider. Meanwhile, they keep shooting at the window, and Avshal presses himself against the wall near the storage cabinet. Through the crack, Tal spots four armed terrorists. He shouts at Avshal that they must surrender.

We have mere seconds to decide. After a split second, Avshal concedes: There is no choice. We decide to surrender. We can already hear grenades exploding outside. The terrorists might throw a grenade inside at any moment and wipe us all out. Avshal and Tal raise their hands above their heads, and Tal shouts in Arabic, "*Waladi, waladi!*" *There are children with us.*

The terrorists ask, "How many?"

"Six," Tal answers, counting the women with the children.

We stop resisting. Avshal opens the steel panel on the safe room window. We are totally mute. Tal climbs out first through the gaping hole. Avshal follows.

That will be my last glimpse of my beloved partner in life.

We, the women and children, crawl out from under the bed. It takes time. "Jihad! Jihad!" the terrorists shout at us, yanking us out one by one through the window. One of them spots my glasses on the desk, where I left them for safekeeping while I was lying on the floor. In a rare moment of humanity, or perhaps this was a lesson of their rigorous training, he hands the glasses to Adi, who is the last to leave the safe room, and she passes them to me.

Outside, the terrorists hold Naveh and Yula in their arms and begin marching away from the house, into the unknown. Adi—my heroine of a daughter, a lioness of a mother—does not flinch. She runs to fight for her babies. Through the chaos, her eyes lock onto Yula, only three years old, some sixty feet ahead. One of the terrorists is holding the child the way one might hold a toddler, a gesture of domestic calm warped by terror.

When Yula spots Adi over the terrorist's shoulder, she reaches out with her small hands, wordlessly begging for her mother. In that moment, Adi does not calculate the risk; she simply runs and seizes her daughter.

The terrorist yanks the girl back, and Adi erupts into a primal scream: *"Mother, child! Mother, child!"* A horrific tug-of-war ensues, Adi pulling, the terrorist pulling back, a desperate struggle for a precious little life. Finally, the terrorist relents, and Adi nearly crushes Yula against her chest.

But the nightmare is not over. Thirty feet ahead, Adi sees her little boy, Naveh. Another terrorist is clutching him by the arm, leading him away. Naveh's back is turned; he cannot see his mother, but his terror is etched into his miniature frame.

Once again, Adi runs. Once again, she engages in a soul-shattering tug-of-war, her voice hoarse as she screams that same haunting mantra: *"Mother, child!"* She refuses to let go. Driven by a raw, bodily instinct that bypasses all logic, she manages to hoist both children onto her waist, one on each hip. The children are heavy, but Adi carries them with a strength born of pure desperation. She does not weigh options or fear consequences; she knows only that her children belong in her arms, and she has just pulled them back from the brink.

With AK-47s pointed at us, we are shoved along the familiar paths of the kibbutz toward what is now the perimeter non-fence. Barefoot and in our pajamas, we are forced into the grueling trek toward the vehicle that will whisk us into Gaza.

Out of the corner of my eye, I see six or seven neighbors lying shot on the sidewalk near our house. In a cluster. Like they went out for a walk and were murdered together. I feel like I'm watching a movie. This feels surreal. I'm emotionally detached. I dare not turn my head. I dare not try to work out who they are.

A fierce flash of envy ripples through me. *They* no longer have to face what's coming. For *them*, it is over. *They* won't suffer anymore. *They* won't have to make fateful decisions. *They* won't have to try to cope.

And us? We are being herded like sheep into the terrible unknown.

Dozens of terrorists walk along the central path of the neighborhood, armed with staggering amounts of firepower. Their swagger tells me they have conquered the kibbutz. They roam around my beloved neighborhood like they own the place, striding between the bodies of my friends, certain they have all the time in the world. It is as if they know what we do not: For hours to come, the Israeli army is not going to come to save us.

Loaded with rifles and grenades, the terrorists drive us toward the breach they made in the kibbutz's perimeter fence. One of them, short and scrawny with crazed eyes, tries to cuff my hands behind my back. I gently try to evade him, pulling my hands forward before he can bind them. I look pleadingly into the eyes of the older terrorist leading us, silently begging him to save me from getting cuffed. He tries but fails to stop the younger, crazier one from binding my hands. I am the only one they cuffed.

They shove us forward with brute force, weapons at our backs. Out of the corner of my eye, I see Lilach and Tari's house. A bomb must have gone off inside. Half of their roof has collapsed, and black smoke is billowing from inside. The chances they survived are extremely slim, maybe 1 percent, but I still pray their safe room kept them safe. Maybe the terrorists failed to break in.

We move as if sealed in a glass bubble separating us from reality. My attention turns inward, to survival, to keeping us alive. There is no room for feelings. Not even for grief. Not for our loved ones, not even for ourselves.

We continue toward the breach in the fence and see a red car on the other side, a battered old jalopy they just brought in from Gaza. The terrorists force us into the car. First they shove Sharon and Noam into the back seat. Then me and Naveh, who immediately sits on my lap. Then they cram in little Yula. There is almost no space left for Adi. Every split second is critical. Every hesitation can mean death. Every moment of doubt might separate her from her children, who are already inside. The terrorists are tense and jittery. The car starts rolling with the door still open. Adi forces her way in, squeezing onto half of a car seat, and a terrorist violently slams the door behind her.

Two terrorists take the front seats. The car drives off, along the same route as my morning walk, between the beautiful fields and orchards of Be'eri, going west, toward the border.

A sudden realization washes over me: There is no point thinking about our former life. My flight to the Netherlands that evening, the Fair Planet meetings, the presentation of our new training booklets. It's all gone. It is futile to look back.

I draw on insights from literature. I think my ability to grasp this sudden switch in real time, to focus only on the immediate task of survival, is shaped by a book I happened to be reading just last night, the biography of the famous sculptor Chana Orloff, the sister of my maternal grandfather, Zvi Nishri. The book, *Sculpting a Life* by Paula Birnbaum, describes Orloff's escape from occupied Paris in 1942 with her disabled son, Eli, the moment the local arrondissement police commander tells her that she is on a list of Jews to be handed over to the Nazis the next day.

That portrayal of Orloff's abrupt fall from celebrated, avant-garde artist to homeless Jewish refugee, determined to save her child and her future, resonates with me deeply. It helps me understand the radical change we have been thrust into, even as we roll toward Gaza, trapped in the terrorists' car.

From now on, every fiber in me focuses on survival, moment by moment. On the here and now. I stare straight ahead. All of us, including the children, are silent. From inside the moving car, I see the countless Gazans—armed men and civilians alike—who flooded Be'eri, looted belongings, and are now carting them back into Gaza with shouts of joy. Some are riding stolen bikes. Some are walking. Others are driving mobility scooters piled high with spoils: bags, televisions, laptops, and so much more. An unthinkable caravan of theft and plunder.

I don't turn my head. Naveh, that tender child, will later describe how he saw bullet-ridden bodies lying along the roadside. The car keeps driving, passing the plowed field primed for potato planting, moving on toward our mango and avocado groves, crossing wheat fields. It travels along the familiar beloved roads and reaches the ANZAC Memorial overlooking Gaza City, built to commemorate the soldiers from Australia and New Zealand who were killed in First World War battles between British and Ottoman imperial forces in 1917.

There, on the paved area by the tall observation tower, the terrorists stop and radio their headquarters, asking where to take us. They fumble for a few minutes, then turn right and north, toward Gaza.

The drive is effortless. There is no border, no barrier, no ditch, no soldiers on the ground, no air force overhead. There isn't even any visible marker of any boundary between Israel and the Gaza Strip. This surreal reality, so utterly different from everything we were promised for decades, is painfully seared into my heart.

Near the crossing, one of the terrorists tells us, "Welcome to Gaza," and unthinkingly, I answer, "Thank you."

Anxiety consumes us.

We are in the Gaza Strip.

CHAPTER III
HOSTAGES

Saturday, October 7, 2023, 11:00 a.m.

THE TERRORISTS' CAR TURNS INTO Gaza's narrow alleys. We sit rigidly in the back seat. People in the street react with ecstasy as the driver honks and excitedly announces his spoils: Six hostages crammed shoulder to shoulder in the back. The cuffs are biting into my wrists behind my back; my fingers have begun to go numb.

We drive deeper into a densely built neighborhood. The poverty is crushing. Even after more than twelve years working in some of the poorest regions of Africa, I witness a different kind of poverty here. In the villages where Fair Planet works, the poverty is extreme, but at least the alleys and paths are clean, anything that can be reused is recycled, and the small mud houses are decorated with murals. Yet here, in these cramped streets, I behold squalor. Trash piled in the roads. Dilapidated buildings. Palpable neglect.

We keep zipping through the alleys, and each mound of trash nearly stops the rickety car. As we drive, I think again about the nonexistent border we just crossed. If there had been any physical obstacle in our way—a ditch, a berm, anything—it would have been far harder for the terrorists to snatch and steal us into Gaza. In hindsight, it is obvious that any physical barrier would have meant fewer hostages. Right now, we still have no idea how many there are.

At a certain point, the car stops beside a building on the right, and the driver gets out. I assume he is going to consult someone about where to hand us over, and to whom. The second terrorist seizes the chance, now that we are alone, and "asks" us to give him our jewelry. Adi removes a gold earring and hands it over; Sharon gives him a delicate gold necklace, along with twelve-year-old Noam's colorful fabric bracelets. With my hands still cuffed behind my back, I slip off my wedding ring from my right hand, a three-color braided gold band, and I pass it to the terrorist with Adi's help.

On my left hand, I have a diamond-and-sapphire ring my mother inherited from my grandmother and gave me as a wedding present. Passed down through generations, this precious ring is especially dear to me. It was made of platinum in early-twentieth-century Germany, in a distinctive Art Deco style. It is oval-shaped, with fourteen hand-polished natural diamonds around the perimeter. In the center is a larger diamond, surrounded by delicate filigree work, and on either side of the oval are four blue sapphires.

Before traveling to dangerous areas of Africa with Fair Planet—*how ridiculous that name sounds now*—I usually take the ring off. I hide it somewhere in the house and send Avshal a photo of the hiding place, just in case I don't come back. But this time, my flight on October 7 was booked to the Netherlands, a safe destination. So I left the ring on.

Now, I decide: *I'm not handing it over.* I know this is dangerous, irresponsible, and irrational, but I am determined they will not steal my family's heritage from me. My hands are still cuffed behind my back, so the terrorist cannot see what I am doing. In ordinary circumstances, I need soap or moisturizer to get the ring off. But now, with tremendous effort, I wrench it off my finger and shove it under my pajama pants, hoping to snag it on the inner seam of my underwear.

Here too, I am thinking of the book about Chana Orloff. When she fled France with her disabled son, she was joined by her close friend, the painter Georges Kars. As they made their illegal passage across the Swiss border, they had to ford a raging stream. Kars's coat, where he had hidden his family's jewelry to secure his future, fell into the depths and was lost forever. In all his years living as a refugee in Switzerland, he could never shake off the loss.

The fate of my ring, which for me symbolizes the intergenerational continuity in my family, will similarly haunt me for many years to come.

The driver returns to the car, and I ask him to release the cuffs that have practically paralyzed my hands. He agrees, and at last my hands are free. We keep driving through the crowded streets until the car stops in front of a house. We are ordered out and told to walk into the yard, close to the wall and under the trees, to avoid detection by the IDF's aerial surveillance.

I feel like I am in free fall. Like Alice in Wonderland, tumbling past a strange, shifting kaleidoscope of realities, reacting in each instant to whatever flashes into view. That's me now. Focused on survival, minute by minute, then another minute, and another.

Saturday, October 7, 2023—the first apartment in captivity (one day)

We are smuggled inside. The two kidnappers transfer us to a three-man guard unit, all armed from head to toe but dressed in civilian clothes.

Inside, the house looks half empty. We are led into a small room with a blue double sofa and a large cardboard box full of toys. The realization hits me like a blow. The toys were prepared in advance. *They planned to kidnap little children and hold them as bargaining chips.* How psychotic. What devilish cruelty. How inhumane to abduct toddlers as pawns! And how unprecedented.

The terrorists separate me from my family, move me into an adjacent room, and leave me there for a few minutes that feel like hours. There is a cage holding a small yellow canary hanging in the room. *There is life here.* I stare at the bird, so tiny and fragile, in its cage. *You and me too?* Despite my fears, nothing happens, and before long, they bring me back to the others.

We are tense and extremely anxious. Communication with the guards is extremely limited. They barely know English beyond a few words, which they probably learned as part of their captors' training: *Bomb. Far. Food. Come. Go.* We do not speak Arabic. Ironically, the only sentence I remember from high school is: "*Fi yawum wahad, khatafuha dhi'b.*" *One day, a wolf abducted her.*

I understand I must conquer my rage and terror to achieve one singular mission of shielding my family from these monsters and their twisted, malicious values. I look at Naveh and Yula, so young, so delicate, so innocent, and I know: I must not lose control. I cannot show weakness. I must look the terrorists directly in the eyes, never lower my gaze, display no emotion. I must project only determination and inner resolve.

From the moment of our abduction, my role is clear to me: *I am bringing everyone home alive.* I say this to nobody but myself, over and over. This is my mission.

Watching the terrorists, I identify the commander. He seems to be the oldest, around forty. Medium height. Not fat, but his belly is starting to round. A high forehead. Short brown hair with early signs of balding at the crown. His full face is framed by a carefully trimmed mustache and beard. Thick lips. He speaks with authority, and the other two seem to accept his command.

The second terrorist is lean, sturdy, and muscular, with a round, boyish face and no mustache or beard. The third is also lean and sturdy, with thick black hair, a short mustache and beard, and discerning eyes.

At one point, a woman arrives, covered head to toe in a black burqa, only her eyes visible through a narrow slit. In fluent English, she explains that we have been abducted as bargaining chips to secure the release of their prisoners from Israeli jails. There is not a trace of criticism or even the slightest hesitation in her description of the criminal act of kidnapping small children as "leverage." She cooperates fully with the terrorists. She shows no compassion or warmth toward the children, neither in her eyes nor in any gesture. She tells us she will search our bodies and notes that after she leaves, we will remain only with the men. But they will not harm us, she adds.

I do not know whether to believe her. Either way, I realize she will inevitably find the diamond ring hidden in my underwear, and I ask to go to the bathroom. Inside the tiny stall, I search desperately for a way to get rid of the ring to save it from ending up in the terrorists' hands. At first I wrap it in toilet paper and throw it into a small trash can beside the toilet. Then I reconsider. I fear they will search the trash, a fear that later proves justified. They check every scrap of paper and anything else we throw away.

Then I notice a tiny cabinet built into the right wall, with a yellowish plastic door. I open it and find bottles of cleaning supplies, and behind them, water pipes. I wedge the ring, still wrapped in tissue paper, into a gap between the pipes and close the door.

The woman searches us, shielding our privacy from the men, and gives us clothes so we can change out of the pajamas we were abducted in. I receive black sweatpants with a pocket on the right, a skin-colored tank top that serves as a bra, and a cream-colored, sequined sweatshirt branded CASTRO, a popular Israeli brand. Adi receives a gray leopard-print T-shirt and black pants. Sharon receives a dark blue tunic and black leggings.

The children are left in the same clothes they were kidnapped in.

After we change, the woman asks our names and ID numbers, where we are from, and which medications we need. Because of a recent surgery on my left eye, I need eye drops three times a day. She promises I will receive the drops the next day, and I do.

On our first night in captivity, they take us to the second floor of the house, which is empty of furniture. They bring the children the toybox from downstairs, arrange mattresses on the floor, and tell us where to sleep. They position themselves in the adjacent room, facing a wide doorway left fully open, and, armed with rifles and grenades, watch us closely. To calm the children, I tell them that the men are there to guard us.

The children play with the dolls from the box: a large, soft Winnie the Pooh and two blue Smurfs. One Smurf has a white mustache, beard, and red hat. They decide to call him Fufu. The other is Papa Smurf, with white hair, thick eyebrows, a long mustache and beard, and a yellow hat. They call him Huli. The two Smurfs keep my grandchildren company throughout their captivity, almost until the last day before our release.

But cute dolls cannot erase reality. The threat around us is clear. Fear forces us to focus only on the here and now. Everything narrows down to survival, moment by moment. Every reaction must avoid showing weakness.

I remember an article from *Science* years ago that described what a newborn experiences at birth. The mother's contractions press the baby through the birth canal, and the baby must focus on the single most important process to their survival: pumping blood from their heart to their brain. The other organs receive almost no blood because they are less vital at this stage. That is why many babies are born with bluish hands and feet.

That's us now—focused only on what is vital to our survival.

I remember few other details from that first day in captivity, but I recall with certainty that even then, I knew that my family and all our friends in Israel would scramble into action and that they would do whatever it took to secure our release. I was sure they would turn the country upside down.

I do not yet comprehend the full scale of the disaster of October 7, but I know the attack on Be'eri was unprecedented. I know the terrorists conquered the kibbutz, murdered men, women, and children, blew up and burned homes, and abducted us from our beds, barefoot and defenseless.

I also know that the army and the state abandoned us on that fateful day. The battle cries I heard from inside the safe room were only in Arabic. The gunfire I heard came from the hopeless defense waged by Be'eri's emergency squad. Just eleven civilians, trying to defend us against more than three hundred terrorists swaggering around the kibbutz, drunk on victory.

With my own eyes, I watched a pogrom being inflicted on us by barbaric terrorists, and we had no defenders or saviors. Just like those cursed days before Israel's independence, over in faraway Ukraine, in Russia, in Germany, all around Europe and across the Arab world.

I know my father's family history from conversations with him and his parents. Abraham Havron was born to Edgar and Aanna Heilbronner, who lived in Stuttgart, Germany. My grandfather Edgar (Yaakov) was an orthopedic surgeon who worked for a government health clinic; my grandmother Aanna (Chana, née Rothschild) was a family doctor. Shortly after the Nazis rose to power in 1933, my grandfather was dismissed in accordance with the law to fire all Jews, including doctors, employed by the state. There was one exception: Doctors who had served at the front with the German army in the First World War were safe from dismissal. My grandfather petitioned the authorities to keep his post under this clause. He was told that although he had served as a military doctor and had even received the Iron Cross, his surgical work as a military orthopedist was too far removed from the front lines. His request was denied, and he was fired. My grandmother, who had served at the front itself, applied for his position, but Nazi officials gave her a polite German refusal. Their explanation was that she had been a nurse during the war, and only after the war did she complete her studies and qualify as a doctor.

The closing of those doors opened my grandparents' eyes. They were not Zionists. Their Judaism consisted of going to synagogue on Rosh Hashanah and Yom Kippur. But they understood Jews had no future in Nazi Germany and decided to move to the Land of Israel right then, in 1933. That was how they saved their lives and that of my seven-year-old father. The Nazis and their accomplices would later murder almost our entire extended family in the Shoah.

My maternal grandfather, Zvi Nishri, and his family survived pogroms in their hometown of Starokostiantyniv in southwestern Russia (now Ukraine). I learned about them only recently from the book about his sister, Chana Orloff. The Jews there suffered brutal persecution, and the pogroms were proof of their vulnerability as a helpless minority. This reality pushed my mother's family to leave their homeland and join the effort to establish the State of Israel.

But us? Born into an independent state with an army that was considered one of the mightiest in the world, we always assumed someone would protect us. That our existence was not in danger. Then reality strikes, literally and figuratively. The Israel Defense Forces did not come to rescue us—neither the ground troops nor the air force—just as in Russia generations earlier, my family had no redeemer. Rage and helplessness flood me in the face of this cruel betrayal.

Sunday, October 8, 2023—the second apartment in captivity (5 days)

As darkness falls, the terrorists give us, the women, hijabs to cover our bodies and our heads. They leave only our faces visible. They also provide us and the children with plastic flip-flops and then drive us to a second house.

This house belongs to a senior Hamas figure and his family. They place us on the second floor, and to separate us from the family, they assign us a small room of our own. Our captors use masking tape to hang an improvised curtain between our room and the rest of the apartment. They bring three mattresses and prop them up against the wall. On one wall is a large window, covered with an opaque fabric to hide us from people on the street outside.

On another wall hangs a poster depicting jihad against Israel. On a map of Israel labeled "Palestine," armed terrorists are shown in an attack position around the Gaza Strip. To the right of the center of the map, near Jerusalem, is a circle with a magnified view of the Temple Mount and the Al-Aqsa Mosque, with flames and columns of smoke covering the entire country.

I cannot help but note the irony that the map on this poster resembles the one Benjamin Netanyahu presented in his speech at the UN General Assembly on September 22, 2023, just two weeks before the October 7 attack.

Our captors position themselves in the entryway between the front door of the apartment and our room, armed with a vast amount of firepower. They set up a makeshift filming station and record us with a GoPro. Their commander, holding the camera, hides his face with a black balaclava. I imagine the mask is there to prevent viewers, including Israeli security forces, from identifying him from the reflections in my eyeglass lenses. The terrorists dictate what we must say: our names, ID numbers, criticism of Israel and Prime Minister Netanyahu, and a demand to release their prisoners.

When they instruct us to say we are being held by Hamas, I feel a certain relief, because until that point, we have no idea who actually abducted us or who is holding us. At least it's not

Islamic Jihad, who are even worse. At least it's not random civilians, because then we would be lost forever. This is the first moment I tell myself: *OK, we have a chance of getting home.* I know Israel has channels of communication to Hamas, so there will be negotiations for a deal, just like the woman told us yesterday. Eventually, we will be released in exchange for their prisoners.

The terrorists also demand our Facebook account details and email passwords so they can send messages to Israel supposedly from us. I decide to give them the email address of Amnon Tamir, Fair Planet's chairman and head of IT. I draft an email for them to send him from me. In my phrasing of the subject and the message itself, I try to warn him that there may be a virus, which I suspect they want to send, and to signal that the content was dictated to me.

Behind the makeshift curtain, we can hear the voices of the man of the house and his wife, and the sounds of children laughing, shouting, and playing. But they are all out of sight. The homeowner brings our rations to the door near our captors' post, knocks, and leaves. Our captors pull the food in, bring us some of it, and eat the rest themselves.

They demand we stay quiet, whisper at all times, and keep away from the street-facing window, especially when the street fills with people returning from prayers at nearby mosques. When IDF airstrikes begin, they explain in very basic words where to find "the safest place there is" in the apartment. We use the same phrase in Israel to describe possible shelters from Qassam rockets. Only here, there is no reinforced safe room or concrete shelter. Here, the "safest place" means staying away from windows and pressing against an interior wall.

They also tell us that in an emergency, they will allow us to move under the improvised curtain into the adjacent room, further from the window. At one point, I steal a glance through a narrow gap between the curtain and the wall and see it is the family's living room—spacious, with a rug in shades of red, burgundy, and black, surrounded by black upholstered sofas. I notice the family's children are banned from the living room while we are held behind the curtain because the flimsy partition would obviously not hide us from them.

After this introduction, we pulled the three bare mattresses from the wall, arranged them across the floor of our cramped quarters, and readied ourselves for sleep. We lie down in the same order we will adhere to throughout our captivity: Yula pressed against Adi, Naveh at my side, and Noam huddled against Sharon. Our feet are pointed at the street-facing window, our heads toward the entryway. The terrorists insist our door remain open at all times so they can watch us around the clock, and they leave the light in the entryway on all night. The cold fluorescent glare makes it hard for us and the children to fall asleep. To help them, we find some small items of clothing and gently place them over their eyes. When we notice that they have shifted during the night, exposing their gentle faces to the light again, we adjust their makeshift eye masks to block it.

Three days after we arrive at this house, the guards receive a report of a "roof knock" warning aimed at a building two doors down from us. "Roof knocking" is a procedure the IDF uses when it has reasons to believe that uninvolved civilians may be inside a building marked as a target for an airstrike. First, Israeli soldiers call the inhabitants to warn them of an imminent strike. Second, to make sure they leave, they fire a small munition near the building or onto the roof, and only then do they drop the bomb that flattens the building.

After the report of a roof knock, our captors order us into the corner farthest from the window facing the house that is expected to get hit. It is at this point that tensions begin to surface within our small group of three women. A silent but highly fraught struggle emerges over where, exactly, to shelter the children, since the room's safest corner can only accommodate one. Meanwhile, the homeowner and the chief captor hold up two mattresses with their bare backs facing the window, exposing themselves in order to protect us, their precious bargaining chips. This is the only time we see the man of the house, whom I believe to be a senior Hamas commander. We hear the impact of a falling bomb nearby. The windows shudder but remain intact; within minutes, our captors return to their posts.

Two more days pass. Anxious dread. Uncertainty. Survival.

Friday arrives. Our first Friday in captivity. The street sounds different from a weekday. No honking, no construction, no vendors hawking their wares. We hear muezzins calling people to Friday prayers through powerful loudspeakers and crowds flocking toward nearby mosques. The sermons sound aggressive and frightening to me, the tone threatening. From time to time, I pick up the words "Israel" and "*Yahud*" ("Jew"), and I understand they are calling for revenge.

That evening, another roof knock warning arrives, this time on our building or the one next door. We expect about fifty minutes between a warning and a strike. As soon as the warning comes, the terrorists scramble to evacuate us and the homeowner's family. They gather up the mattresses, drag all of us out into the street, and lead us through the darkness about 330 feet away from the building. We reach an awning, and they position us under it with the mattresses held up in front of us, facing the street. I am standing at the edge of one mattress, when I suddenly feel a small hand take hold of mine. It's a child's hand, the child of the man holding us captive in his house, the child of a Hamas officer. Such a simple, human gesture in a moment of terror and deathly fear.

When the warning time passes and the sounds of the bombardment fade, the terrorists waste no time checking whether the building they are holding us in was damaged. They squabble among themselves for several minutes and decide to move us elsewhere. They don't seem to have prepared a backup plan. A car parked nearby signals to us with its headlights. Again we cram into the back seat and get driven off. We maintain absolute silence. After a few minutes, we reach a low, dark office building. Our captors consult with their comrades on the phone—and lead us to our next destination.

Saturday, October 14, 2023—the third apartment in captivity (one day)

After a short drive, the car stops in front of a house. The terrorists go inside to speak with the owner. We are left alone in the car, in anxious anticipation. Escape does not even cross our minds. There is no chance we would survive on the hostile street. No hope anyone would come to our aid. Some forty-five nerve-racking minutes pass. In hindsight, I realize we are being held up so they can move the inhabitants out before bringing us and our captors in.

We are ordered into the house and taken to a little girl's bedroom. Everything in the room is pink, with Hello Kitty everywhere. What unbearable dissonance between this innocent child's sweet little room and our reality: helpless, frightened, captive. Threatened by weapons that could cut our lives short at any moment.

The terrorists leave us in the Hello Kitty bedroom and go to the living room for another long consultation. We hear them arguing and trying to persuade someone. Maybe the homeowner does not want us there, but eventually the matter is settled, and we stay for one night. They let us take cold showers in the bathroom that is also covered in Hello Kitty accessories: a mirror, a hairbrush, hair clips. I think of little Yula in this absurd situation.

The next day, the man of the house enters our room and introduces himself as Abdullah. He sits beside us and, in relatively fluent English, angrily recalls a time an IDF soldier insulted him at a checkpoint before Israel evacuated Jewish settlers from the Gaza Strip in 2005. Abdullah used to work in the greenhouses of one of the Israeli settlements, and at the end of the day, he returned home through an army checkpoint. It was already late, and the soldier told him the crossing was closed and he would have to sleep in his car. According to Abdullah, the soldier threw him a sarcastic "Good night." Nearly twenty years later, the humiliation is still seared in him, and now, from his place of power, he wants to shame and humiliate us. We listen in silence until he finally leaves.

As evening falls, Abdullah announces we must move to another house. "Very safe, very safe," he says. Later, we learn this house also belongs to a senior Hamas family. He points to the hijabs hanging on hooks on the wall to the right of the entrance and orders us to wear them over our clothes. When we walk in the streets, we must look like Gazan women and not arouse suspicion that we might be hostages. He also gives us plastic flip-flops and instructs us to go outside, into the dark street, and walk in absolute silence in pairs, each pair escorted by a terrorist.

I go first with Naveh. Behind us is Adi, holding Yula. Then Sharon and Noam. The dark street is practically deserted. We walk several dozen yards, are led into a courtyard, and then begin climbing stairs to the second floor. Naveh needs the bathroom, and one of the terrorists carries him quickly up the stairs in his arms. I lose sight of him. After a few seconds of panic, we see Naveh emerge from the bathroom, and we can breathe again.

We settle down for the night.

Sunday, October 15, 2023—the fourth apartment in captivity (43 days)

I wake up early, scan the spacious apartment, and discern that it belongs to a well-off family. Soft carpets cover the living room floor; the windows are covered in two layers of curtains: one opaque and one sheer, embroidered with flowers. A lavish chandelier hangs from the center of the ceiling, made of clear glass panels centered on an array of small bulbs shaped like candle flames.

In the living room is a table with a vase of artificial flowers, a green velvet couch, three small round tables, and modular sofas composed of luxuriously embroidered cushions in a variety of shapes. The black fabric on the upholstery is threaded with silver and red leaves. A thought suddenly flashes through my mind: My mother, who mercifully died before the disaster of October 7, would have loved this fabric arrangement.

On both sides of the living room stand bookcases with glass doors framed by carved wood. Both also function as partitions: One separates us from our captors' room, the other from another room that we cannot see into. The shelves are packed tightly with books, some carelessly stacked in a heap, and it is clear the books are actually read and not just on display to impress.

On the living room wall hangs the same poster we saw in the second apartment depicting jihad against Israel. Naveh looks at it and asks what it shows. Because the poster is relatively dark and the living room is usually dimly lit, we try to wriggle out of answering, hoping he will miss the details and not understand what it means. But this eight-year-old boy, who witnessed similar scenes of horror when we were forced out of our safe room, who saw our friends lying dead, who looked straight into the terrorists' murderous eyes, who watched houses in the kibbutz going up in flames, understands that the poster represents the terrorists' desire to destroy the State of Israel.

Two other photos hang on the wall. One shows an elderly, respectable-looking man with an elongated, wrinkled face and long white hair and beard. The other shows a baby a few months old, with sweet round cheeks and fine hair spiking like a hedgehog's quills around his head.

There are three windows around the living room: one large window with ornate glass panes facing a busy square and two small ones overlooking a very narrow alley and facing the neighbors' apartments directly opposite. Our captors warn us not to approach the windows when the lights are on, to speak only in whispers, and to stay clear of the innermost window, which is only about three feet across from the neighbors' balcony.

Here too, the partition between us and our captors' quarters stays open at all times, and they watch us around the clock. In rare cases, they close it to prevent us from seeing what they are doing, such as when they clean their vast arsenal of weapons or when an outside visitor comes to call.

Our captors explain where the safest place in the apartment is, reigniting the tension between us about where each of us will sleep. The arguments are fraught and highly charged. I realize it is my job to mediate, to mollify, and to put my foot down and make a decision for all of us when necessary.

The Israeli bombardments intensify as night falls. They are terrifyingly close; the noise is literally deafening. Often, when airstrikes hit right by the apartment, the walls shake and the windows rattle. The children are paralyzed with fear. So are we. We adults all grab cushions from the seating area and try to cover the children's bodies and our own heads. We know the cushions offer no real protection, but it is the only active thing we can do, and it gives us and the kids a sense of safety, even if imagined. We wake up and doze off in cycles all night.

The four terrorists are unruffled by the bombardments. Three of them snore softly in their sleep. One, on watch, stays awake listening to a crackling transistor radio.

Before we reached this apartment, our captors' team consisted of the same three terrorists. Here, they were joined by a fourth. They all call each other "Muhammad," to hide their identities from us. Later, Adi manages to figure out their names from slips of the tongue and eavesdropping on their calls, but we never dare let on that we know.

The new Muhammad is very thin and relatively tall, with a slightly hunched posture, trimmed black hair, dark eyes, and a short mustache and beard. He moves in and out, rearranging our living quarters and hanging a blanket over the translucent partition between us and the rest of the apartment. In time, we understand he is the homeowner's son. He also speaks English well, and the communication between us and our captors improves significantly.

Adi scans the bookshelves, scrutinizing the covers with Arabic titles, and suddenly spots a book in English: *Principles of Medicine*. This must be a doctor's home.

I understand that communication with the homeowner's son—and, through him, with the other captors—is critical to our chances of survival. From now on, for the next forty-three days, we will subsist in a tiny sealed universe.

Six hostages and four captors, forced into a world in which every interaction between each of us and our captors—and the dynamics between ourselves, the hostages—will play a monumental role in our struggle for survival.

CHAPTER IV

WE ARE THE SAME

WE HAVE NO CONTACT WITH the outside world, neither practically nor emotionally. We are completely hidden. Everything beyond the narrow corners of the apartment where we are allowed to stay is a hostile zone. I think of us like a group of astronauts in a spaceship flying through a ruthless universe; only, unlike a real spaceship, this one is full of terrorists pointing their guns at us. Our lives depend on their every whim. The threat around us is constant, ever-present. The only thing that matters is staying alive. Nothing else.

The bathroom is the only place we enjoy privacy, if only fleetingly. In the small vestibule leading to it is a tiny sink with a cold-water faucet, above which hangs a broken mirror. Inside the bathroom itself, to my surprise, above the toilet bowl, is a cistern made by Lipski, an Israeli company. We must fill the tank by hand, using a large plastic bucket our captors bring us.

On the cistern lid sits a bottle of Keff shampoo, another Israeli brand. The name means "fun." How surreal to see Hebrew in the heart of hell. How useless. There is also a shower in the bathroom, but our captors forbid us from using it.

The bathroom is the only place where we can let out emotion, anger, and frustration; the only place we can cry freely, away from the eyes of children or captors. But even there, all throughout my captivity, I do not cry. I fear crying will crack the hardened armor I have donned. It will weaken me, make me fall apart.

Above the toilet is a tiny street-facing window, and we can hear the people outside clearly. But cloistered in here, we must remain invisible, unseen and unheard by the terrorist's family living on the other side of the partition in the same apartment, by the neighbors just across the alley, and by the crowds in the street. We know that if we are discovered, we will be eliminated.

Life inside this tiny capsule becomes the center of our existence. I can hardly bear to think about Avshal and Tal, I believe they were both taken hostage and are being held somewhere in Gaza. Since we surrendered together, I cling to the hope that they are alive. Adi and I try to sustain one another and keep that hope alive. As for everything else—Lilach, Tari, and the horrors in Be'eri—I force those thoughts away and focus only on the survival of the family I have with me.

And in the depths of this carnage, I feel a fiery jealousy unfurling within me toward anyone the disaster passed by. I picture most people in Israel watching the news, clicking their tongues—*Isn't it terrible what happened to those people on the Gaza border?*—and then going about their daily lives again. Identifying with our plight for a moment, then moving on.

Only after we are released, after fifty days in Gaza, do I understand just how powerfully whole swathes of Israeli society identified with us, how they mobilized, and how they struggled with all their might to get us out of captivity.

We give each of the Muhammads a nickname: "Commander Muhammad" (the oldest, the one in charge), "Kid Muhammad" (with the round, boyish face), "Nice Muhammad" (with the sensitive, intelligent eyes), and "Homeowner's Son Muhammad," or for short, "Son Muhammad."

Son Muhammad brings the children toys and drawing books emblazoned with the logo of the United Nations Relief and Works Agency (UNRWA), the Palestinian refugee agency. And I think to myself: *Is this really the UN's only contribution to our wellbeing?*

Our captors operate highly professionally, positioning themselves and their weapons caches in the most strategic part of the apartment, controlling the entryway and keeping constant watch over us. There are no cell phones. From time to time, we hear the ringing of a landline and incoming and outgoing calls. We often gather they are speaking with Abdullah, the owner of the "Hello Kitty" house. We do not know what the connection is between them, except that his home is very close, about 100 to 130 feet from the apartment where we are currently being held. I assume that he is a civilian, and because he agreed to "host" us for one night, he is in on the secret of our location and is therefore a kind of threat to our captors, obligating them to answer his calls.

At some point, about three weeks after we arrive at this apartment, the landline breaks. The terrorists bring a screwdriver set and try to fix the wiring, but to no avail. From that point on, there is no phone communication at all. I assume they are passing messages to their headquarters through couriers. Son Muhammad comes and goes freely because his errands and grocery runs do not arouse the neighbors' suspicion. The other captors rarely go out, however, for fear of drawing attention to what is happening inside.

The conditions in captivity are harsh. Beyond the constant life-threatening danger and the deprivation of freedom, food is scarce and hygiene is dismal. Showers are strictly forbidden. At most, once a week, we are permitted a meager wash using a single 1.5-liter bottle of water per person. On colder days, the captors occasionally agree to warm the water for the children, granting them a second bottle for their wash.

We receive only one towel between the six of us, so whoever washes first gets to use the stiff towel while it is still dry.

We decide the children will always bathe first and rotate between them. Whoever finishes passes the towel to the next person; by the time it reaches the last of us, it is already heavy and soggy. We wash in the narrow bathroom stall. I go in to help Adi bathe Yula, who grows scrawnier as captivity drags on. The sight of her breaks my heart and saddens me to my core. To shorten her misery and the time she is stuck in the cold, after Adi soaps and rinses her, I wrap her in the towel and hold her until Adi finishes combing through the knots in her hair with a couple of drops of conditioner, gently washing her hair with a little water and goes to fetch her clothes.

Naveh is still wearing the Hapoel Be'er Sheva soccer shirt he was abducted in. On the inside tag is Hebrew writing, and when our captors take our clothes to wash them, I am suddenly seized by panic that they will hang the shirt out to dry with the tag facing outward, giving away our hiding place.

Gripped by anxiety, I go to Son Muhammad and ask him to make sure the tag is not visible. Amused, he explains that almost all the clothes in Gaza have Hebrew tags because many of their factories manufacture for the Israeli market.

Later, the terrorists hand us plastic bags with a change of clothes, and we try to match them to the children, both by size and by appearance. After that, we choose for ourselves from the leftovers. Sharon pulls out a dark blue tunic with tiny white dots embroidered on the fabric. I fish out a burgundy tunic with white Bedouin embroidery. Adi takes out a gray shirt with "Female is the Future" stitched across the front from the Israeli brand Daniella. We look at each other and think how ironic the slogan is: Here we are, hostages in Gaza, where women are barely allowed to leave the house, and if they must, then they have to wear a hijab covering their heads and bodies, leaving only their faces visible.

From the sounds coming from the other side of the apartment—children's laughter and crying, occasionally a man speaking and a woman answering—we deduce that the homeowner and his wife must have four or five children, including two little ones. The mother clearly knows how many "guests" they are putting up, and I wonder whether she also knows we are hostages held against our will. At first, I still believe she might think we are Hamas operatives evacuated from another house. But that doesn't square with how they force us to whisper all the time. So she must know we are hostages.

Usually we get three meals a day, at random hours, prepared by the mother in her kitchen and brought to us by Son Muhammad. I notice our captors eat the same food in much larger quantities. As for drinking water, there were no rations—we could drink as much as we needed.

The meals are inconsistent. Sometimes they are relatively varied; other times, there is nothing nutritious to eat, which creates friction between us. In any case, we decide the children eat first; only then do we, the adults. To reduce the tension, I take charge of rationing whatever is in short supply. If there are vegetables, I count the cucumber and tomato pieces and give each child one third. Naveh does not like *labneh*, so I split it in two by tracing a line down the middle of the white lump, half for Yula and half for Noam. And when there is fava bean stew, which the children like less, we eat a little more than usual.

At some point, we realize they have started bringing us our breakfast quite late, and Naveh, who is used to waking up early, goes hungry until it arrives. The first few times, we hide some small pieces of flatbread for the children; only a few days later do we dare to ask the terrorists if they will allow us to hold onto two or three from dinner to solve the problem. They oblige.

Before October 7, I was a vegetarian and had not touched meat in decades. But my mission in captivity is to stay strong as possible to function as well as I can, so despite my revulsion, I decide to eat whatever they serve me, knowing at least that Muslims also avoid pork.

One evening, they bring the children some bags of chips. Of course, the children devour the snack. Three days later, with only one bag left, our captors tell us, "You should know, this is the last bag of chips left in Gaza." We decide immediately not to touch it, feeling it would be wrong to have something that the children of Gaza cannot have. To avoid tempting our children, we hide the packet behind the small water container on the table near the window. Later we debate whether to offer it to the children beyond the partition, the homeowner's children, but we fear it could be perceived as shaming them. But these are the first few days of captivity, before the hunger truly begins to set in. At this stage, despite the fear and the unknown, our conscience prevails.

As the days bleed into weeks, the luxury of such moral debates vanishes, replaced by the stark reality of scarcity. The terrorists tell us there is a food crisis in Gaza and that the IDF has struck the pita bakeries. The shortage reaches us too. The mother, whom we never meet, is forced to improvise meals from leftovers. She cuts dry pita ends into cubes, for example, and adds them to lentil soup to create something filling from the little she has to play with. On another day, when even lentils are out of stock, she serves flatbread triangles toasted over an open flame with olive oil and za'atar, with some fresh flatbread on the side. And I keep telling Son Muhammad, again and again, to convey my thanks for the cooking and for the hot, sweet tea we get with almost every meal.

One day, an argument erupts between me and our captors. I cannot recall what exactly it is about, but tensions run high. Dinner time has already passed, and I fear they will not bring us food at all. At some point I go to the bathroom, and when I come back, before I even have a line of sight to our quarters, I tell our captors that it is already very late and the children need to eat. Son Muhammad answers, "No, there is no dinner today." I protest and demand that they bring food for the children. Then I see they are smiling. They already served us dinner while I was gone, and everyone has already eaten except me. The tension dissipates. He simply enjoyed worrying me.

The days go by, and the terrorists miss no opportunity to share information about the worsening shortages in the Gaza Strip. It's a transparent attempt to make us feel guilty about Israel's response to the crimes of murder and abduction perpetrated on October 7. They want to shame us, as if we have any sort of influence over Israel's actions.

Then the terrorists tell us about a severe fuel shortage in the Gaza Strip. They joke that people are forced to walk or to rent carts pulled by horses or donkeys, and that the prices for these animal taxis have skyrocketed. But Hamas itself has unlimited fuel, with fully-loaded cars at their disposal throughout our captivity. They are clearly stealing fuel intended for civilians, just as they steal their food.

As our days in captivity stretch on, my understanding solidifies that Hamas could not care less about its own civilians. Consumed with hatred for the entire Western world, they are focused on the mission of global jihad: to destroy and devastate Israel first, then advance the global spread of Islam. The masterminds of Hamas' unprecedented October 7 invasion—those responsible for the slaughter, incineration, and abduction of civilians—knew full well that Israel would respond with all its might to fight for its survival and the return of its hostages. Their strategy was as cynical as it was cruel. By operating from within densely populated areas, they ensured that any Israeli response would inevitably impact Gazan civilians, allowing Hamas to shift global scrutiny away from their atrocities and toward the resulting suffering in Gaza.

Furthermore, our own captivity is an integral part of this malicious calculation. By holding us within private family homes, they use us as human shields. They understand that the IDF will refrain from striking locations where hostages are known to be, effectively turning our presence into a personal shield for the captors and their families.

Our captors give the impression of being deeply devout. Commander Muhammad usually prays five times a day, and the younger men usually join him. Before each prayer, they perform their ablutions, washing their faces, hands, and feet at the tiny sink in the corridor leading to the bathroom, and the foot-washing ritual leaves dirty puddles on the floor. After washing, they kneel on small prayer rugs, facing east. That is how we know where east and west are.

I look at the terrorists' bare feet as they pray, at the fine creases in the arches turned toward us, and reflect on how vulnerable they are, how much they remind me of the feet of barefoot toddlers. My thoughts drift to the mothers who once beheld those feet when these men were still babies.

Once a week, our captors clean our room, and for this, they move us into theirs. To my surprise, they all roll up their sleeves equally, including the commander. On one of the armchairs in their room, I notice a small pillow covered in black and gold sequins, the kind you can brush with your fingers to change the color. Kid Muhammad shows the children how to draw a smiley face on the pillow, gold on black, and then the reverse. The children take turns doodling different shapes and stroking the soft, sparkling pillow.

While we wait, I look around and see photos of three people who resemble Son Muhammad hanging on the wall. At the bottom is Arabic text and a symbol I do not recognize. At first I try to convince myself these must be photos of him at different ages, but that thought is quickly replaced by another conclusion. These must be three of his brothers who became *shahids*—"martyrs."

It dawns on me we are being held in the family home of Hamas zealots, a family who sees the deaths of their sons on the altar of jihad as a noble sacrifice. I remember learning that in the Islamic tradition, martyrs are promised seventy-two virgins in paradise. It's a tradition that glorifies death, that promises believers a future reward to encourage them to devote their lives to waging jihad and to accept death with a coolness of mind, if not a certain lust.

My levels of fear and anxiety rise.

And yet, despite our terrible predicament, I am sustained by the firm belief that we are going to make it home safely. I cling stubbornly to the hope that we will walk free because the State of Israel will give Hamas nothing if the women and children are not released to safety.

***

Morning hours are the hardest psychologically. Another night of bombing has passed, and we awake from a night of fractured, broken sleep into this cruel reality, this existence of helplessness and uncertainty. To ease our pain, even slightly, I go to Adi and Sharon almost every morning and tell them, "Every day we make it through safely, every day we survive brings us closer to getting out of here. I don't know how long it'll take, but we're getting out of here in one piece."

When dealing with our captors, I am determined to be the go-between, to put myself on the front line as a buffer between them and my family. I feel that is my responsibility as Adi's mother, as the grandmother of the two small grandchildren who came to visit us that cursed Saturday and were pulled into this hell, and as the sister-in-law of Sharon and aunt of little Noam, who purely by bad fortune chose to stay with us on that terrible day.

I come up with a series of mat exercises and work out for about half an hour every morning. I need to protect my body and soul and project strength. I make myself eat whenever I can, whatever there is, and sleep whenever I can.

Around us, the Israeli airstrikes are terrifyingly close, and I try to fall asleep by humming to myself the "Palmach Anthem," an old pre-independence marching song, like a mantra. *Sleep, so you won't think. Sleep, so you will live.*

Though the storm is ever raging
Still, we raise our sights afar.
Give the order, we'll obey it,
The Palmach, that's who we are!
From Metula to the Negev,
From the front to your backyard,
Every youth, go grab your weapon!
Every youth, stand on your guard!

Only now, as I write these lines, do I understand how Zrubavel Gilad's words, written in 1941, are still relevant to our harsh and cruel reality. Around us, a storm is ever raging, yet nobody stands guard over us. The orders never come; no youth with weapons flock to our rescue from the Negev.

I make a point of keeping track of the day of the week and the date. Following the days of the week is not too difficult. The sounds of the street change on Fridays, when Muslims do not work, and a relative quiet prevails outside as the sermons from the mosques become louder and more frequent.

But knowing the date is harder. I am helped by the memory that I was set to take part in an "open day" in Rwanda as part of Fair Planet's work, scheduled for Wednesday, November 15, 2023. Knowing that November 15 falls on a Wednesday anchors my sense of time. It lets me connect the date to the day of the week, and so I manage to keep track of the calendar.

It so happens that we prepared the invitations for the open day in advance, as usual, and scheduled them to send automatically from my email account to our partners around the world about two weeks before the event. Only after we are freed do I discover that the email was sent. It causes a wave of panic because I am already a hostage. One of our Dutch donors, who knew of my situation, forwards the email immediately to a close friend of mine in Israel, and she urgently sends it to the National Cyber Directorate. After a thorough check, they conclude the email is harmless, and the panic subsides.

***

In our first days in captivity, Israel's military response in Gaza comes only from the air. Endless bombings, always at night. It's terrifying. Out of habit, every time a bomb explodes near us, we leap to shield the children with cushions. Then Son Muhammad tells us this is pointless. In Gaza, he explains, they teach children to clap when they hear a bomb. If they can hear it, it means the bomb did not hit them, and if it hit them, they won't hear it anyway.

I tell him he is right because the speed of sound travels at over one thousand feet per second, and the sound of the explosion does indeed arrive after the impact.

Every time a bomb falls nearby, our captors jump up and calm the children right away, sometimes with a piece of chocolate, a lollipop, or other sweets, all to stop the children's frightened voices from exposing our hiding place. Over time, we become familiar with the odd candy-toys beloved by children in Gaza, like a cardboard cell phone with a "battery" of compressed sugar, twisting gummy snakes, and a spinning top with a candy hidden inside.

In the early days, we are all in shock and barely speak because of the order to whisper. But in the doctor's house, the days stack up, and the sense of routine weakens the children's discipline. So I invent a small dance with the words, "We have to be quiet, quiet, quiet. We have to be quiet, quiet, quiet." *Sheket, sheket, sheket.* I emphatically whisper "*sheket*," every time, waving my hands left and right, and spelling out the letter *shin* with my fingers. With this little ditty, I keep reminding the children of our captors' instructions.

They almost always manage to even stifle their crying. Little Yula sobs silently; only her appearance reveals her distress, and we try to soothe her without speaking. And I think to myself, where did this tiny girl learn to hone her instincts to a point that in her deepest frustration and sadness, she can smother her sobs? Back in the good old days, we used to marvel at how her small body could produce such a loud cry, it felt like it could blow the ceiling off. And now she understands, even wordlessly, that her life is in the balance.

Naveh and Noam find it harder to hold back, especially when they are overwhelmed, and sometimes they cry out loud. In those moments, we panic. We fear how our captors' might react, and we fear that people in the street might discover our hiding place, which would end with us getting lynched. We ask the kids, if they must cry out loud, at least don't cry in Hebrew, so they won't arouse suspicion. We hope their crying will sound just like that of the homeowner's children, which we often hear beyond the partition.

Our captors keep telling us that the IDF must not find out where we are "because it wants to kill you and us together." We do not believe them, but we keep as quiet as we can and stay away from the windows. Sometimes the street outside suddenly surges with life. We hear crowds running and shouting, and that freaks us out. Our captors rush to the window to see what is happening, and usually, though not always, they try to calm us. "No worry, no worry."

Beyond the risks of aerial bombardments and the hostile locals in the street, I am scared of a possible IDF rescue attempt. It is clear from the outset that such an operation would be hopeless. I remember the attempt to rescue Nachshon Wachsman, kidnapped by Hamas in 1994. When Israeli special forces, Sayeret Matkal, stormed the house where he was held, the terrorists killed him, and they also killed the commander of the rescue force, Nir Poraz. In our case, given our captors' high level of readiness and the fact we are women and children, I reason the chance we would survive a similar operation is precisely zero.

Over time, I notice our captors stop closing the windows all the way, even on very cold days. They insist on leaving them ajar, about four inches on each side, which makes the wind blow the curtains aside. I realize they leave the windows open so the shockwaves from the airstrikes will not shatter the glass.

Throughout this entire period, we hear IDF drones buzzing overhead. This buzzing lasts almost all day, its volume changing depending on the drones' proximity to our location. Our captors are fully aware of these patrols, and unlike us, they can tell the different models apart from the engine sounds.

From their reactions, I get the sense they believe the Israeli aircraft are gathering information not only through imagery but also by listening to what is said inside apartments, whose windows, as I have said, remain open at all times.

Almost every morning starts quietly. The sounds of war fade, except for whirring of the drone overhead. No fighter jets, no bombings. The streets around us begin to pulsate. People go about their business, buying, selling, fixing things up. We hear cars and carts, and vendors hawking their wares: *"Alkulur, alkulur!"—Chlorine, chlorine!*—just like the junk dealers back home. Hearing is the only sense we can rely on to understand what is happening outside.

And then, almost every afternoon, there is a fixed ritual. Rockets are launched from a position near us, from the direction of the mosque, toward Israel. From the loudness of the whistle as the rockets fly past, we learn to distinguish between those fired at the border communities and those aimed at the Tel Aviv area. The rockets fired toward the Tel Aviv area, which is further away, take off with a much louder roar, but they are rarer.

When evening comes, the Israeli fighter jets return, and the bombings resume around us. When I was a teenager, there was a saying in Israel: "The best boys to the air force, the best girls to the pilots!" Now, lying on a mattress on a bare floor, with my grandchildren beside me, their lives threatened by those same pilots, I remember that slogan and tell myself that our "best boys" are bombing us.

The bombings draw closer and closer. The fear of death is stifling, and our minds race. *Will we even live to see morning?*

In time, I conclude that this "game"—their rockets in the afternoon and our bombing at night, over and over—is leading nowhere. For all of Israel's aerial might, the air force alone is helpless to lift us out of this heart of darkness.

***

In our first days in the doctor's house, I dare not look outside. The large window is covered by two curtains. In daylight, when the chandelier lights are off, our captors pull aside the blackout curtain and leave only the sheer one. When darkness falls, they close the blackout curtain again; only then do they turn on the lights in the apartment.

After about two weeks, I notice our captors occasionally drop their guard. When the wind shifts the curtains aside, I stand cautiously near the window at an angle I think will not draw their attention and peer out.

That is how I begin collecting details about our surroundings.

The apartment where we are imprisoned faces a rectangular square, ringed by dusty asphalt roads, with a large shopping center on the left side. There are usually several cars parked in the middle of the square, and along the road closest to us is a small line of trees. During the day, the square is quiet, with few people, cars, or carts. Across, about three hundred feet away stands an eight-story building painted a pale cream, with burgundy balconies. Sometimes I can make out women hanging laundry on their balconies. Ordinary life. They are free, and we are captives. Sometimes it looks like one of the women is glancing our way, and we are seized with dread that she might spot us.

The days pass, and our interactions with our captors become more meaningful. For a long time, really until the day of our release, I assume our captors were a relatively junior unit, so I attach little importance to the snippets of remarks they throw our way.

Sometimes Kid Muhammad talks about their goals in abducting us. Because he knows only a few words in English, he mimes. *You*, the civilians, will go home in exchange for a cease-fire, and *they*—he taps himself on the shoulder to signal military ranks—will be exchanged for our prisoners.

Suddenly, I understand we share the same interests. They need us alive to maintain their leverage for a truce, and we need to survive so we can go home. The interests are identical; the reasons could not be further apart. And in order to survive, it is the human relationship we forge with them that will protect us from them and from the many dangers all around.

At one point, I dare to ask Kid Muhammad whether "civilians" includes civilian men. *Yes,* he answers. That gives us hope that Tal and Avshal will also get out, because we believe they are also in Hamas captivity. The terrorists do not tell us what happened on October 7 or how many hostages they have, and we do not ask.

I gather that there is no way we were the only family abducted from Be'eri. I assume two or three more families from the kibbutz chose, like us, to surrender rather than be murdered, and now they are hostages too.

Back when we were forced out of the safe room, when I saw dozens of armed terrorists roaming through our neighborhood, bodies sprawled in front of my home, it was clear to me that they had conquered Kibbutz Be'eri. Nothing like this had happened since the War of Independence in 1948. But here in captivity, we have no idea about the scale of the massacre in the other Israeli communities on the Gazan border; we have no clue that *hundreds* of Israelis are being held by Hamas, Islamic Jihad, or so-called "unaffiliated" Gazan families.

***

Every few days, Abdullah comes to visit us in the apartment. He badgers us with his bellicose talk, claiming, for example, that the IDF is committing crimes and that Hamas will conquer Israel, while our captors try to keep him away from us with a range of excuses.

Throughout this entire period, our captors sleep in a separate room from us. During his many visits, sometimes Abdullah decides to stay the night on the green sofa inside our quarters, which feels oppressive and threatening.

Abdullah also violates what little privacy we have in the bathroom, the only place the terrorists do not constantly watch us. Sometimes we wash our clothes in a basin on the bathroom floor. We do laundry in pairs to minimize the time we are away from the children, and while we rinse and wring, we talk to each other. Abdullah, hearing our conversations, aggressively demands that we remain completely silent, claiming people in the street can hear us. We have to obey, but later I understand that because we are on the second floor, nobody could have heard us from the street anyway. He did it simply to ruin the few minutes when we felt slightly free of the terrorists' control.

After our release, it becomes clear that Abdullah is no mere neighbor who agreed to "host" us, but a senior Hamas operative—with a uniform, rank, weapon, and everything—who served as part of our captor team.

***

My conversations with Son Muhammad become routine. We sit and talk at length nearly every day, usually late in the evening. I note to myself that he is one of the people with the most acute emotional intelligence I have ever met. And I think, if only he had been born into a different reality, if only he had received a different education, he and his friends could have developed their abilities and built better lives for themselves and their families. They could have become people who strove for peace, a bridge in the service of harmonious coexistence.

Everything comes down to education.

Even though the conversation is, on the surface, between two equals, we both know exactly where the power lies here. I am a hostage held by force with my family. And he, despite his civilian clothes, is a Hamas operative with a weapon who controls every aspect of our lives and our fate.

In one of these conversations, after I thank him for looking after us and ask him to convey my thanks to his mother for her cooking, I muster the courage to voice my pent-up anger about the terrorists who stormed Kibbutz Be'eri, murdered people, burned homes, and abducted civilians. I tell him, "I cannot bear what those Hamas militants did in Be'eri. I saw it with my own eyes." And then he replies with the sentence that has never let go of me since:

"We are the same."

"We," not *you and us.* "We" meaning *us and them.* We are the captors and they are the murderers. We are like them. We are all just doing our jobs.

What a powerful sentence. What a cruel sentence. Even out of captivity, I still cannot absorb or confront it. There is simply an unfathomable dissonance between the connection we feel we are forming with our captors—as we spend hours in conversation, while they feed us, guard us, and connect with the children—and that horrible statement, *"We are the same."*

The same as those who slaughtered my friends in Kibbutz Be'eri without mercy.

"We are the same." Son Muhammad says it calmly, as if it is a fact I need to understand, or maybe even a kind of apology (to himself, to us?) for the fact that they are not "real fighters," only "hostage babysitters," without any battlefield heroism, without all the action.

I do not respond. I freeze for a moment. I understand exactly what he is saying, but I cannot find words to respond. And I know that even if I find them, I will not be able to bring myself to say them out loud. I sit across from him. The conversation continues as if nothing was just said, as that formative sentence was not just uttered, one that expresses the total identity between him, the man sitting cross-legged and at ease in front of me, and the terrorists who invaded our homes and committed those barbaric atrocities.

Only after I walk free can I grapple with the meaning of those words. Only then can I understand the evil inside that sentence. To understand that indeed, *they are the same.* To digest what he was really telling me:

> *If I were in their place, I too would have murdered like them, taken hostages like them, burned houses like them. Right now, I'm taking care of you because you are an asset, and because in exchange for you, we can get a ceasefire and the release of Hamas' prisoners out of Israel.*

And inside that sentence is another brutal subtext:

> *If anyone tries to rescue you by force, or if we receive the order—I too will kill you.*

CHAPTER V
THE CHILDREN

THE UNRWA NOTEBOOKS THE TERRORISTS bring the children begin to fill with their drawings. Naveh, the ever-talented, draws what he saw when we were kidnapped from Be'eri. In comic-book style, he sketches terrorists firing their weapons in every direction, with speech bubbles coming out of their mouths.

Adi and I panic at the thought that our captors might see what he is drawing, and we cajole him into turning the rifles into sticks with flowers poking out. It reminds us how absurd our situation is as hostages: We are asking an eight-year-old to completely transform the message of his drawing so the terrorists will not take revenge on us. And it suddenly strikes me how much our request mirrors the symbolism of Isaiah 2:4: "They shall beat their swords into plowshares, and their spears into pruninghooks; nation shall not lift up sword against nation, neither shall they learn war any more."

The notebooks become a source of immense tension because we know the terrorists will carefully inspect anything written in them. We scrub out words, alter drawings, and rip up any pages that might endanger us, lest our captors think the illustrations are mocking them.

After we are released, Naveh draws a series of pictures showing armed terrorists riding jeeps or Hamas men striking violent poses, and writes "I HATE YOU." He also becomes something of a gun enthusiast (toy guns, of course) and walks around with them, pretending to shoot people in his way. You don't have to be a psychologist to guess that he is trying to regain a sense of control after being in such danger for fifty days.

Yula also doodles in her notebook, and we follow the development of her skills with interest. From simple drawings of basic shapes, figures of people gradually take form: Big round heads on top of stick-man bodies. I am glad to see that she usually draws the faces with a smile. Maybe it is a sign that despite everything we are going through, she still sees the good in people.

In the first days, Yula stays glued to Adi all the time, but she slowly begins to join Naveh and Noam in their activities, while always making sure she has eye contact with her mom. From time to time, she asks for some privacy to be alone with Adi, and to make that possible, we use two corners of the modular furniture to create a kind of little cell, one that hides her and Adi from our captors' eyes and gives them some brief moments of intimacy and grace.

***

In our first days in Gaza, I suspect our captors are following a manual for holding child hostages and possibly even getting advice from a child psychologist. Every time there is a crisis in our tiny detention space, whether from an airstrike that rattles the building or when the children get especially upset, one of the terrorists, usually Son Muhammad, immediately enters our room and pulls some kind of candy out of his pocket. This happens so often that the children nickname him "Dessert Muhammad."

The terrorists also bring the children cardboard cell phones, with a "battery" made of candy and printed emojis representing the dialer, contacts, messages, and so on. For us adults, receiving toy phones only underlines the absurdity of our total disconnection from the world. But the children enjoy these new toys. They pretend to call each other and their friends, while our captors can check off a box on their child hostage protocol sheet.

The monstrosity of planning to kidnap children, the depravity of their detailed preparations to hold them hostage, ripping them out of their parents' arms at gunpoint and dragging them like wild beasts into Gaza—all of this goes so far beyond the boundaries of human morality that I cannot wrap my head around it.

It is only a year after our release that I learn what Adi kept to herself all that time. On that horrific day, one of our kidnappers had made their intentions chillingly clear: "Women and children, go; men, boom boom."

It hits me like a ton of bricks. Throughout captivity, as we cope with this nightmare together, Adi never shares this piece of news with me, so I won't lose hope. And there I am, still projecting confidence whenever I can that Avshal and Tal are also hostages in Gaza. We both try to keep each other strong, to avoid doing anything that might weaken the other woman's spirits.

That horrific sentence—"Women and children, go; men, boom boom"—proves again what lies behind the toybox that greeted us on our first day in captivity: Hamas concocted its devilish plot to kidnap children well in advance.

One of the things the terrorists let the children do, as part of their protocol, is to play hide-and-seek. It requires no equipment, and thankfully, it suits Yula too. It is hard to hide in such a small space. But with enough childish imagination and creativity, the children pull it off, hiding in the corners, under the long curtains and blankets, behind the green sofa and side tables, or under the table with our water pitcher. Sometimes Yula "hides" simply by closing her eyes, and in her mind, she becomes invisible.

Even Fufu Smurf and Huli Smurf are full partners in hide-and-seek. One of the children hides them, and the others must uncover where they are.

One day, Son Muhammad, who we know has younger siblings, joins the game with the children. Other times he plays hide-and-seek with Yula for hours on end, with a patience reserved only for people who truly love children.

On another occasion, Naveh decides to hide in our captors' room. They chase him out in a panic because they hide their weapons and grenades under the sofas.

When hide-and-seek loses its charm, Son Muhammad brings us a deck of cards. We sit in a circle to play Cabo, and as I deal out the cards, my mind wanders to the first time I ever played this game, somewhere in Asia.

Avshal and I had decided to fly with Shaked to meet Adi, who was hiking through India. Yuval did not join because he was traveling in Australia at the time. After an exhausting journey, including a long flight to Mumbai and an overnight train to Jaipur, we met Adi after months apart. We excitedly hugged, heard her stories, and were quickly swept up in the spirit of freedom. We decided to travel together through that colorful, fascinating land.

One evening, in a hotel somewhere, Adi asked if we knew how to play Cabo, a game that had become a hit among young backpackers in Asia. When we said no, she explained the rules: The game is based on memory, strategy, and luck. Each player gets four face-down cards and is allowed to look at only two of them. The rest of the cards remain in the draw pile, and each player can draw a card and decide whether to swap it with one of their own or discard it. Cards eight and above allow you to peek at a competing player's card or swap with them.

If you think you have the lowest total value, you can declare "Cabo!" and then the others get only one more turn to try to lower their points. After that, everyone reveals their hand, and the winner is the one with the lowest score.

The game is challenging and fun, and we get hooked.

From that wonderful flash of memory, I force myself back to the present, and our game of Cabo begins.

Playing cards becomes a meaningful activity for us, and some of the terrorists join from time to time. It turns out they are extremely competitive, even when they are playing against children aged twelve and eight. They jot down the results on paper and calculate who has won each round.

Over time, the cards wear out, and some develop creases that let anyone with a sharp memory know, just by looking at the back, what number is on the front. That is cheating, of course, and the children, who quickly pick up on these clues, decide not to use them to keep the game fair. Then they point out to us that Kid Muhammad is using the same clues to win. It is equally infuriating and amusing, but we all know who has the guns, so we bite our tongues.

When we are sick of Cabo, we move on to play War or Memory with the children, and they almost always beat us, the mothers.

Son Muhammad also brings us Connect Four. It is a thinking game for two participants. Each participant gets tokens, either red or yellow, and takes turns dropping a token into a board with seven columns and six rows. The goal is to connect four tokens of the same color in any line before your opponent. This game is suitable for Yula too, and it keeps the children occupied for long stretches of time. The tokens also serve as money when the children later decide to stage a play and sell tickets to their captive audience, pun intended.

One day, the terrorists bring the children some bubble toys, and they blow bubbles throughout the room. At a certain point, Commander Muhammad joins in too, even though he rarely plays with the children. To our great surprise, this burly, threatening terrorist turns out to be a real virtuoso with soap bubbles. He makes enormous ones and shows the children how to bat the bubbles into the air and catch them again with the loop at the end of the bubble wand.

Then he takes the game up a notch: He blows a huge bubble, bounces it toward Naveh or Noam, and they "catch" it with their wand and bounce it back to him, again and again, until it pops.

We know Commander Muhammad has small children, and I think to myself, *What a terrifying synthesis*: He has such a human touch with the children, but here he is, holding all of us hostage with weapons loaded to fire at any moment.

At one point, our captors bring the children a small ball and suction-cup basketball hoop with a net, one that sticks to the wall. The children start playing, and the ball accidentally hits a picture, a portrait of the man with gray hair and a long beard, on the opposite wall. To our horror, the picture, dangling from a single nail, hits the floor. Son Muhammad notices immediately. He storms in, his body language projecting fury, but he does not say a word. He picks up the picture and takes it to the other side of the house, to hide it from view. I wonder who the man in the picture is. A religious leader the family follows? The father, the man of the house himself?

The passageway from our room to the bathroom runs past the bookshelf partition, which is almost always left open. About once a week, our captors close the partition so they can clean and oil their weapons. In the first weeks, they are meticulous about closing it while they work, so we will not see the weapons, but over time their caution slips.

One day, Noam, who needs to use the bathroom, crosses the open partition and suddenly sees a row of Kalashnikov rifles laid out on the floor. She runs back to our room in panic and asks me, "Why do they have so many guns?" I know immediately that I must not tell her the truth: Those weapons will be used against us if step out of line or if Israeli forces try to rescue us.

But I still have to give her an immediate explanation that will reassure her and let her continue living in her world of make-believe. "Are you kidding?" I ask her. "They're guarding us! Who's ever heard of an unarmed guard? Just like in Israel we have armed guards in malls to protect people. It's the same here." The explanation seems to satisfy her. The incident does not repeat itself.

But we, the mothers, have no illusions. The message was delivered loud and clear with those words: "We are the same."

After about a month in captivity, Yula whispers to Adi that the terrorists knew we were hiding in the safe room in Be'eri because they heard her crying there. This precious child, only three and a half years old, has been carrying this burden of guilt in her heart for all those weeks. I can't wrap my head around it.

"That's not true," Adi explains. The terrorists knew we were home because they saw our unmade beds and the cups of hot chocolate on the kitchen counter, still full because the children had not had time to drink them. "It's not your fault at all, sweet

Yula." My wise little granddaughter accepts the explanation and breathes again, while we ache over the fact that at such a tender age, she was carrying such an unbearable weight until she summoned the courage to open up.

***

Throughout captivity, we are constantly trying to invent new distractions and activities to keep the children occupied. One that comes to mind is a game of make-believe. On November 16, 2023, the day after I was supposed to fly to the open day in Rwanda, I ask the children whether they sensed I was acting strangely the day before. When they ask why, I answer that the woman who was with them yesterday was my double, because I had to fly to Rwanda. After all, it would be unthinkable for the keynote speaker not to show up at the open day.

The children burst into a barrage of questions:

> *But how did you get out of here?*
> *How did you get to the airport?*
> *How did you fly to Rwanda with the war all around us?*
> *How did your double get here?*
> *And how did she know how to behave in captivity?*

I explain that indeed, because of the war, I could not get to Ben Gurion Airport, so I had to leave Gaza by hovering. I point to the chandelier hanging from the center of the ceiling and say that I simply vanished through it and continued flying, floating all the way to Rwanda. There I joined my team from Israel and played my part at the event, which was a roaring success.

I tell them that my double entered through the chandelier, just as I had left, so as not to arouse the terrorists' suspicion that

I had disappeared. I add that the night before, I invited my double here and taught her what is allowed in captivity (speaking only in whispers) and what is forbidden (going near the windows, asking our captors questions, and so on). The only thing I could not teach her properly was the card games, especially the tricks of Cabo.

I tell them how, when the open day ended, I bade goodbye to the guests and flew back, hovering once again, and slipped down through the chandelier straight into the room where we are being held hostage. "Didn't you notice that yesterday you beat the one you thought was me at Cabo more often than usual?" I ask them.

The story of the hovering double ignites the children's imagination. They take it and run with it, telling each other how they themselves hovered off to some faraway place.

Only weeks after I am released, when I finally have the time and emotional wherewithal to reflect on what we endured in captivity, I recall a film by director and actor Roberto Benigni, *Life Is Beautiful.* The film is a tragicomedy about the Holocaust of Italian Jewry. The father, Guido, played by Benigni himself, hides the severity of the situation from his son, Giosué. When Giosué asks why there is a sign in the storefront reading "NO ENTRY FOR DOGS OR JEWS," the father explains that it is the shopkeeper's preference, and that in another shop he saw a sign barring Chinese people and kangaroos.

Unlike the insights I gleaned from Holocaust memoirs, which help me consciously steer my behavior in captivity, I am oblivious in real time to the inspiration I took from Benigni's film about easing children through days of imprisonment in a hostile space with mortal danger lurking all around.

Another activity that occupies the children, one of their favorites, is a play they devise themselves. They call it *"The Adventures of Yigaloni and Naima: The Inept Criminals."* Noam and Naveh are the writers, producers, directors, set designers, and actors in this spectacle. Naveh plays Yigaloni, and Noam plays Naima. We ask them to include little Yula too, and they give her the role of ticket seller and seat usher for the audience. The children decide that payment for the show will be made with tokens from the Connect Four game, and that the entry tickets will be the joker cards from the deck.

Noam and Naveh plan the plot in whispers. They decide that in each act of the series, they, the criminals, will go on an adventure and fail spectacularly.

Their first mission is to rob a bank. They build the set, choose costumes, prepare a backstage area to change outfits as they rotate characters, and before the show begins, they have the audience sign a declaration stating that if the performance is interrupted by an airstrike, they bear no responsibility.

Son Muhammad is intrigued and asks to join the audience. He buys a ticket from Yula, who scans it at the entrance to the imaginary theater using the cardboard cellphone our captors gave her.

The show begins. It is performed, of course, in whispers, and so essentially takes the form of a mime.

The two robbers arrive at the bank, emptying it out into improvised sacks. Then the actors hide backstage, switch roles to policemen, and catch the robbers red-handed. Sometimes the actors get mixed up, apologize to the audience, confer with each other, and correct the scene. At the end of the episode, they bow to the satisfied spectators.

Every morning, Noam and Naveh perform a new act, robbing someplace else, maybe a pizzeria or a falafel stand, and failing. Son Muhammad makes sure to attend every episode, but once, ahead of episode six, the children forget to notify him of the showtime and he misses it. When he shows up for work the next day, he is genuinely upset. "How can I watch episode seven if I didn't see six?" Somehow the crisis passes peacefully.

Then the producers announce they are going to stage the season finale and apologize that such a good series is coming to an end. In this episode, they apologize to everyone they wronged in previous episodes, but they can no longer really remember who. That's how inept they are.

One day, the children decide to stage a "Shoshan Day" in my honor, or as our captors call it, "Shashun Day." When they wake up in the morning, they do my exercises. Yula cuts corners, performing only one or two exercises, but Naveh and Noam are meticulous and do the entire routine, just like me.

After that, they ask our captors for tape, tear pages out of their UNRWA notebook, make imaginary eye-drop bottles by folding paper, and imitate me by pretending to drip solution into their left eyes.

When our food arrives, the children divide it into rations and initially avoid touching it, just like me, instead drinking tea and waiting for someone else to start eating. Before going to the bathroom, they ask if anyone wants to go first, and so on, charming imitation after charming imitation. To be honest, it is highly entertaining to see how they interpret my behavior in captivity.

***

One day, we hear the first rain falling over Gaza, and we smell the scent of moist earth. Ever since my childhood in Be'eri, the first autumn rain has filled me with a feeling of wonder. The water soaking the wheat fields and winter crops. The intoxicating smell of damp soil. The sweet sound of drops tapping on the roof of the house. The view of the lawn and the olive trees in our yard.

My parents, Abraham and Rina, closely monitored the total rainfall around Be'eri, a parched region where every drop that quenches the fields brings joy. My mother oversaw the kibbutz's meteorological service, which measured daily rainfall, and posted the figures on the dining hall bulletin board.

The first rain in Gaza breaks my heart. It floods me with longing for the life I knew before this present horror, longing for freedom. The knowledge that we are only a twenty-minute drive from home crushes my heart and spirit.

I think of my friend Orna Einstein, the field crops manager of Kibbutz Magen, south of Be'eri, in an area even more arid than ours. I picture the joy that washes over her when she steps out into the fields in the first rain and revels in her freedom, the freedom that has been robbed from us.

I tell Son Muhammad about the joy of rain and how farmers on both sides of the border must be moved by it. He tells me that because of the war, farmers in Gaza cannot work their fields and will have no harvest this year. Only after I am released do I learn from Orna that farmers in Israel were also unable to go out to their fields for the same reason.

As winter arrives, the weather turns colder. The children catch colds, and our captors demand that we report any medical problems to them.

After a few days, Adi tells them she thinks Naveh has a fever. They bring a thermometer, ask us to check his temperature every four hours, and keep an orderly record of the readings. In the late afternoon, Naveh's fever rises sharply. He feels very ill and lies on the mattress, exhausted and weak. Our hearts break with worry.

Our captors inform us that they are calling a doctor to examine him. Some twenty minutes later, they ask Adi to don a hijab and come with Naveh into their room. After they close the partition, I hear another person enter and see silhouettes and flashes of light through the glass panes of the bookcase separating our room from theirs. After several long, nerve-racking minutes, Adi and Naveh return. The doctor concludes that Naveh has strep throat and instructs our captors which antibiotics to give him.

Adi tells us the doctor arrived wearing a baseball cap, with a headlamp and a face mask, and examined the boy in the dark, so she barely saw him. He spoke only with our captors, in Arabic, and did not address her directly.

He clearly knew that his patient was a hostage, and from the first visit, Adi suspects that the doctor is in fact the same homeowner in whose apartment we are being held. We believe that they are making us "wait" for his arrival to try to make us think he is coming from elsewhere.

The next day, the terrorists bring the antibiotic, labeled Amoxicillin. Adi is uneasy about following the instructions of a local doctor who ignored her during the examination, but I tell her not to ask questions. He is a doctor, and we must do as he says. The instructions are to give Naveh the medicine three times a day. Our captors take this to mean exactly every eight hours, so they insist on waking Naveh in the middle of the night. The eight-year-old boy, who had hardly ever taken medicine before, manages to swallow it despite the bitter taste, as our captors whoop, *"Inta jaber, inta jaber!"—You're a tough guy!* After twelve hours, there is already a noticeable improvement, and it is clear the doctor prescribed the right medication.

Two days later, Yula also develops a fever. Again, the terrorists call the doctor, who arrives within fifteen minutes, and again, Adi is asked to put on a hijab and take the little girl into our captors' room. The examination is brief, and the doctor prescribes Yula the same antibiotic. It is the first time in her life she has had to take medicine, and it is a large dose with a foul taste.

After several failed attempts to give the Amoxicillin in a small cup, our captors bring a syringe, and Adi tries to squirt the medicine directly into Yula's mouth. Yula is grossed out by the taste, and some of the liquid spills out the sides of her mouth. She starts to cry, but our captors demand that she receive the full dose. So every eight hours, there is a struggle to make her take the medicine. To help, our captors do their best to make her giggle. They teach us their methods in such situations: promise the child a treat immediately after, squirt it into the side of her mouth between the palate and the cheek, and blow *pfffff* directly into her face, which they claim triggers the swallowing reflex.

In the end, we realize it is simply too much liquid for Yula's little mouth. Only when we split the dose into two do we solve the problem. Yula also responds quickly to the treatment, and the fever subsides. We survive another crisis.

A few days later, a rash appears on Naveh's legs. At first, we think it must have been caused by bedbugs, but after a thorough search of the room, including shaking out the mattresses and pillows, we find no sign of them.

Once again, the doctor is summoned, triggering the hijab routine again as Adi goes to the captors' room. The doctor arrives this time within minutes, wearing the baseball cap, face mask, and headlamp, and he again ignores the boy's mother.

After a very brief exam, he gives Naveh half a pill of unknown provenance. To our relief, by the next day, his rash has subsided, and soon it disappears completely. Given the speed with which the medicine was handed over, it is now clear to us that the doctor is indeed the homeowner and that his house contains a whole apothecary.

The squalid sanitary conditions cause skin irritations and chafing, which compounds our suffering. After a few weeks, the children begin scratching their heads, and it turns out that we are all crawling with lice that torment us unbearably. Our captors bring us plastic lice combs, and a daily nightmare ritual of combing begins, which is especially unpleasant for curly-haired Yula. Many more days pass until we finally manage to rid ourselves of this plague.

The terrorists are careful to note the lice problem in their notebook. Throughout this entire period, they document every action and occurrence, and I understand they are passing detailed reports about us, their precious bargaining chips, back to their commanders.

As time goes by, I notice that on the right side of the wall facing the square is a wooden door painted the same color as the wall. A manual sliding bolt keeps it locked shut. One day, our captors are furious about something Naveh did. To frighten him, Son Muhammad tells him that behind the door is a large freezer and threatens that if he misbehaves, he will lock him inside.

We do not believe him, but the threat alone sends chills down our spines.

CHAPTER VI
ANOTHER DAY IN CAPTIVITY

Tuesday, November 14, 2023—day 38 in captivity

TODAY IS AN ORDINARY DAY, without any exceptional events, but I decide to make a mental record around the clock in the hope of conveying how time passes here, day after day, hour after hour, in the insane reality we have fallen into.

At around 1:00 a.m., the rumble of thunder and the roar of heavy rain pounding the house where we are being held mingle with the noise of airstrikes.

In a panic, we keep pulling out the foam cushions we set aside in advance to shield the children's heads, while miraculously, they keep sleeping.

Every time I am jolted out of my sleep, I find myself dragged back into this unimaginable reality. We are being held captive by terrorists, somewhere in the Gaza Strip, less than half an hour's drive from our home in Be'eri.

I feel the cold seeping into my bones and wake up. Despite the pitch darkness, I can see Adi sleeping on the bare mattress laid on the cold floor, cuddling Yula in her arms. Yula's gentle golden locks frame her sleeping face, and her tiny little feet are propped next to my head. On my other side is Naveh, deep asleep, his eyelids fluttering to suggest he is in the middle of an intense dream. Sharon and Noam are sleeping in another corner of the room.

I get up to go to the bathroom and pass the corridor adjacent to the terrorists' room. There is Arabic crackling out of the transistor radio pressed to duty guard's ear, mingling with the gentle snoring of the three sleeping terrorists. There is no more running water in the bathroom, and I refill the toilet tank using the plastic bucket on the floor.

When I return, I see that Naveh has rolled over in his sleep and his legs are resting on my mattress. I gently move his legs and cover him with a blanket. Yula is also uncovered, but I know she dislikes sleeping with a blanket. Still, I cover her tiny legs to shield her against the biting cold, hoping she will not kick the blanket off again.

At 6:00 a.m., or so I estimate, I wake again, this time to the muezzin's call urging the faithful to attend prayers before sunrise. The voices from the loudspeakers of the nearby mosque blend with the rain and the bombings.

I am suddenly overcome with longing and banish the feeling at once. I have to go back to sleep to survive the next day. And the days to come.

When the first light appears, the thunderous bombardments dwindle to a halt. The rain has passed, and rays of sunlight shimmy through the narrow gaps between the curtains. I wake from a dream and try to grasp its finale, to reconstruct the images that flickered beneath my eyelids just moments ago, but it is in vain. Reality slaps me in the face when I look at the ceiling and remember I am in the home of a family of terrorists, with that chandelier above me, whose glass drops catch the solitary fragments of light that seep in from outside.

I reach for the small round table to the left of the bare mattress I was sleeping on, take my glasses, and look around. Everyone except me is still asleep. What are they dreaming about? What will they feel when they wake once again to helplessness, to total dependence on our captors?

Judging by the faint rustling from the terrorists' room, they too are still asleep. I rise from the mattress, in the same clothes I have been wearing for eight days straight. They are sweaty and smell foul; we have no way of knowing if or when we will ever receive a clean change of clothes. Everything is in the terrorists' hands. Our lack of control over the most trivial things, which we take for granted in the free world, is psychologically shattering and undermines our sense of self.

I walk toward the window facing the narrow alley and, through a slender gap in the curtain, see the neighbors' balcony barely five feet away. I wonder about their lives and their daily routine.

I drink two glasses of water from the pitcher on the table. I learned this habit from my mother many years ago, and every morning, as I sip water, I think of her.

Gradually, the sounds of people passing in the street below begin to rise, along with vehicle noises and the jingle of bells on donkey carts. From time to time, sirens wail, probably police cars or ambulances, joined by the banging and clatter of construction workers next door.

Once again, I must pass the terrorists on my way to brush my teeth at the small sink in the corridor near the bathroom. On a narrow shelf above the sink, our toothbrushes sit in a plastic cup, next to a tube of Colgate toothpaste with Arabic text. I never see the terrorists' toothbrushes. They probably take them back to their room after brushing.

Above the shelf hangs a small mirror, cracked on its right side, with rust stains circling its edges. I look at my reflection in the mirror. It has been thirty-eight days since we were abducted. My hair, unwashed in all that time, has lost its softness, and the curls around my head poke out like frazzled wires. I wet my hands with tap water and try to coax the curls into some semblance of order with my fingers. I see my face, entirely deprived of any skincare routine, and think of those bygone days of normal life, when out of habit and reflex, I would reach every morning for my gentle refreshing moisturizer and makeup.

I remember how, on Yom HaShoah, Holocaust Remembrance Day, I used to watch films on television depicting Jewish women being led to the concentration camps. So many times I have thought about them and tried to imagine how they got by in the darkest days in our people's history. How did they maintain their appearance? And what would I have done in their place?

I brush away the thoughts, and the taste from my teeth. On my way back, I see Commander Muhammad and Nice Muhammad kneeling on their prayer mats. For some time now, I have noticed that they both pray more frequently than their comrades. I scurry cautiously behind them and return to our room.

As always, Naveh is the first to wake. He is already sitting on his mattress; his hair, which has grown so long in recent weeks, tousled and wild. He resembles Mowgli, the hero of *The Jungle Book*. My heart goes out to him. He is so sweet.

I ask if he is hungry, and when he says yes, I take one of the flatbreads I saved from yesterday out of a black plastic bag hidden behind the water container.

I return to my mattress and begin my regular routine of captivity exercises. The routine consists of sit-ups, cross-body crunches, pelvic lifts with deep breathing, and scissor kicks. I perform each exercise fifteen times and make sure to complete at least five sets. On especially dark days, even more.

Besides the fact that exercise is the only way I can move my body at all in captivity and preserve at least some level of physical fitness, it also helps distract me from this depressing reality and slightly improves my mood.

In these moments, I find myself drawing on the traits I inherited from my mother, Rina, whose father, Zvi, was the first gymnastics teacher in the Land of Israel. She was a tough woman who projected no emotions but plenty of determination and strength. We, her children, gave her the loving nickname "Sparta." We knew the circumstances that had forged her. She had lost her mother at the age of three and endured a difficult childhood, moving from one aunt's home to another. In 1936, when she was only eleven, her older brother David was murdered by Arabs who ambushed a car transporting workers and guards from Motza Illit to Jerusalem. In the War of Independence, she fought in the defense of Kibbutz Be'eri, and many of her friends fell in battle around her. As the kibbutz's radio operator, relaying reports to senior commanders, she handled the names of the fallen, which must have shaped her profoundly.

Surprisingly, I take little after my father, a naturalist, a sensitive intellectual, and a man of the wider world. I followed in his footsteps when I chose to forge a professional career in the life sciences, but here in captivity, any traits from my father are of little help in coping with the situation.

Meanwhile, having finished his flatbread, Naveh takes the notebook the terrorists gave him and rummages for pages still empty of his drawings. Even at his tender age, his instincts are sharp enough to tell him that we cannot initiate requests from the terrorists. That is why he does not ask me to ask them, either.

I am constantly astonished by the children's precise understanding of our situation. Though no one prepared them for this, they display wisdom and emotional intelligence that help them, and us, survive.

To my relief, Naveh finds a blank page and begins drawing with intense concentration.

Noam wakes as well, stretches, and joins us. I do not know the time, since we have no wristwatches and the two clocks in the bookcase are broken. Based on the time that has passed since the morning prayer, I gather it is now around 9:00 a.m.

I ask the children what they want to do. Their options are limited, but a few exist. We decide to postpone hide-and-seek until Yula wakes, since it is her favorite game. Naveh suggests Connect Four, and they begin playing against each other. Meanwhile, Sharon wakes up, then Adi and Yula. We tidy the room, stack the mattresses we slept on against the wall, and fold the blankets.

I am acutely aware that today is Tuesday, November 14, and that tomorrow is Fair Planet's open day in Rwanda. I remember the invitations we sent to our partners around the world, "SAVE THE DATE—NOVEMBER 15, 2023" emblazoned in large letters. We listed the program, with me as the keynote speaker, followed by other distinguished speakers, and later a tour of the fields showcasing selected vegetable varieties we had tested for farmers in Rwanda.

I wonder which members of the Israeli team are already in Rwanda preparing the site, blowing up balloons in our green-and-white brand colors, buying refreshments for the guests and the farmers arriving from the villages, and planning the tour. Has Alon Haberfeld, who replaced me as the chief executive in 2021—already landed in Kigali? Which hotel is he staying at? What are they saying about me? About us? What do they know? It does not occur to me that Ben Gurion Airport is closed because of the war and that flights are suspended.

I know tomorrow will be especially difficult for me, as I try to imagine the event unfolding hour by hour. The contrast between my former world and our situation here threatens to throw me off-kilter and pull me away from focusing on survival. I collect myself and look around. Landing back in the here and now.

Three of the terrorists have woken by now, while Kid Muhammad, who was on night watch, is still asleep. I notice that Son Muhammad has left our captors' room, and I hope he will bring us breakfast. Indeed, a few minutes later, he arrives bearing a large, round metal tray.

We clear the games from the center of the room, and Son Muhammad bends down to place the tray on the floor. In recent days, the supply of nutritious food—vegetables, cheese, and sometimes even a small fava bean stew—has been dwindling. This morning, the tray meant for all of us holds only a few slices of cucumber, a small mound of *labneh*, several small pieces of flatbread, and a teapot with six hourglass-shape cups, concave at the center, topped with a delicate gold rim. The elegance of the glassware stands in stark contrast to our living conditions and our sweat-soaked clothes, but a thought flits across my mind: *My mother would have loved these cups.*

Once again, I must pull myself away from the temptation to ruminate on my previous life—and return to reality. I pour the tea into the six cups and serve it, still piping hot, to Adi, Sharon, and myself. I set aside three cups for the children to cool. Drinking the hot, sweet tea before eating slightly eases the hunger knotting my stomach and is the most soothing part of the day.

The children finish eating, move to sit on the pile of mattresses, and whisper about what to play next. We mop up whatever is left of the *labneh* with flatbread, wipe away every last drop of moisture left behind by the cucumbers, and pour ourselves the little tea remaining in the pot.

About an hour later, Son Muhammad comes to collect the empty dishes and return them to the other side of the house. I imagine his mother, living beyond the partition, so close to us, receiving the plates scrubbed clean of every last crumb, and I wonder what is going through her mind. What does she think about the fact that women and children are being held hostage in her home? Can she voice her opinion to her husband or son, or must she obey them without question? Or rather, is she a willing accomplice with what they are doing?

The children gather in a corner of the room and decide to play hide-and-seek with Fufu Smurf and Huli Smurf. They soon grow bored, and Noam offers to teach Naveh how to draw animals. Noam has a simple artistic style, and Naveh adopts it in his notebook doodles. Adi looks at the pages and sees that he has been drawing friendly pigs with plump bodies, tiny tails, and round faces with flattened snouts. She comes over to me and whispers anxiously that pigs are considered impure in Islam.

These drawings might offend or anger the terrorists! We ask Naveh and Noam to stop drawing pigs and alter the ones they have already drawn to look like kittens. It requires considerable creative effort on our part.

At some point, Noam and Naveh tire of drawing. Our fear of boredom and inactivity leading to depression forces me to stay alert and avoid long stretches of nothingness. I immediately pull out my winning card for such moments: another round of Cabo, which draws everyone in.

Usually Yula teams up with Adi and they play as a shared hand, but today she asks for her own cards, so we soften the rules. At some point, Naveh grows bored because it is too easy, and he drops out to play solitaire on his own.

I think it is now around noon. We begin to hear sounds from the kitchen, and half an hour later, the smell of lunch wafts our way. Adi and I try to guess what the woman of the house, whom we have never met, is cooking up this time. Lentils with fried onions? Pasta?

We hear the mother calling her family to eat. We have no idea how many of them there are or how old they are; only crying and the sounds of a babyish refusal to eat reveal the presence of an infant. The clatter of cutlery and plates jingles through the partition, and our stomachs cling to our spines.

Soon afterward, Son Muhammad emerges from the kitchen with the metal tray. He stops in the captors' room, sets down the dishes for him and his comrades, and enters our room with the rest. His face is somber; he does not acknowledge us. I have a hunch that our captors have received bad news about last night's bombardments. Perhaps a family member or friend was injured.

Silence scares us more than hostile speech. The slightest event that affects these terrorists could seal our fate, condemning us to starvation, psychological or physical abuse, or death.

I find myself reflecting on what I learned about Muslim hospitality during a trip to Jordan about three years ago. Our guide was well versed in Bedouin customs, and in the shade of the massive cliffs of Wadi Rum, he explained that one of the most important survival rules in the desert is hospitality, even for enemies. A host must provide lodging, food, and drink or find himself condemned by his society. He explained that the custom arose from the harsh conditions in the extreme heat, where oases and water sources are few and far apart, making hospitality critical for anyone who happens to come one's way.

This memory gives me hope that the rule will also guide our captors' behavior.

As these thoughts pass through my mind, Son Muhammad drops off a tray with a bowl of pasta on the floor. Adi and I look at each other. We guessed right. That alone feels like a small achievement.

Despite the meager quantities, poor nutritional value, and monotony of this diet, hunger makes every meal taste delicious. The pasta, served plain, disappears quickly into our stomachs, as do the flatbreads served on the side.

In the afternoon, Naveh suggests playing the "eraser game." The star of the game is a small eraser we found on a shelf in the bookcase. We all close our eyes, and the first player places the eraser somewhere visible but as out-of-place as possible. The others must find it, without giving away that they spotted it. They are supposed to keep searching theatrically, and then pass surreptitiously by the hider and whisper in his ear where the eraser is. Only when everyone has done so does the game end.

In the background, we hear the muezzin calling for the sunset prayer and the street's hum gradually fades. The children grow bored again, and Adi suggests an improvised memory game. On a round plastic tray, she places a random assortment of objects within reach: coins, an eraser, a spoon, a playing card, a die, plastic toys, and folded paper. Everyone must look carefully, memorize the placement of the objects, then close their eyes while she removes one. The first person to identify what is missing gets to rearrange the objects and begin the next round. A few more minutes pass this way.

Suddenly, we hear the terrifying whistle of rockets being launched from around the nearby mosque. The children cling to us in panic, while our captors leap from their room to the street-facing window, look outside, and shout to us, "No worry, no worry, out, out!" Their faces are glowing. Firing rockets at Israel fills them with pride and joy. I am so jealous of those who are still in Israel, close to their safe rooms, who can step out once the danger passes and go back to their lives. We can expect Israeli bombardments tonight in retaliation, and once again, we will be in mortal danger. It has long been clear to me that the terrorists guarding us are using us as human shields, but does Israeli intelligence even know where we are? Will we survive tonight? The nights and days ahead?

Son Muhammad disappears without explanation, and the air fills with the smell of popcorn and the cheerful popping of bursting kernels. Minutes later, he returns with a steaming bowl of popcorn and places it on the rug. The two younger terrorists join us, and all our hands—terrorists, children, and women alike—dive into the bowl, scooping up the popcorn until it is quickly gone.

Son Muhammad crosses back to the other side of the house and this time serves Commander Muhammad an early dinner. Fasting all day, he did not take part in our little popcorn party. I guess it is now a little before 5:00 p.m., since he usually breaks his fast at sunset.

Meanwhile, our captors prepare for evening prayers and unfurl their rugs. Afterward, Son Muhammad goes to the other side of the house and returns with our dinner. Once again, the food is extremely paltry—a few small pieces of flatbread, two chopped tomatoes, a little *labneh*, and a teapot. I must make do with one or two flatbreads, I realize. This will be my entire meal tonight.

After eating, we gather the empty dishes, arrange the mattresses for the night, and try to place them as far as possible from the windows, which are at risk of shattering from the airstrikes' shockwaves.

The children are hoping for another "party night." Every few days, the younger terrorists come into our room after dinner with a treat, sometimes clementines or some other fruit. They call it a "party," and for us, it is a rare chance to let the children eat something more nutritious than flatbread. If there are any clementines left after the children are done, we eat some too.

This is also an opportunity to talk with the terrorists and deepen our relationship. I am acutely aware of the importance of maintaining a personal connection, even under these monstrous conditions. Still, I know with certainty: If the Israeli army tries to rescue us, or if we are discovered by the angry mob outside, they will not hesitate to murder us. Perhaps a personal bond might make them hesitate for a minute or two before pulling the trigger, but any such dilemma would quickly evaporate, and the gunfire would ensue.

Naveh has developed a clever trick to figure out whether or not there will be a party. He asks Adi to take him to brush his teeth early, so that if a party is planned, the terrorists will tell him, "no, no." *Don't brush your teeth—wait!*

After a few days, Yula adopts the trick herself, and they compete to see who can find out first whether there will be a party. For our part, we at least are happy that they are both eager to brush their teeth right after dinner.

This time, however, the children are disappointed. No one stops them on their way to brushing their teeth.

Meanwhile, I am deeply troubled by the fact that there is not a single leftover flatbread from dinner. I deliberate what to do. Should I dare ask the terrorists for two or three more flatbreads for the kids, for when they get hungry at night or early in the morning? I know we will not be sitting together later tonight, and there will be no casual opportunity to ask. I peer into their room and try to read Son Muhammad's mood to see if I might find the right moment. The terrorists are sitting and talking in whispers. They look worried and tense.

Throughout captivity, I rely on an inexplicable intuition about how to conduct myself with the terrorists. What I can talk about and what I must avoid. What I can ask for and what I can't. When to be firm and when to project ease. I know that every choice I make in dealing with them will affect our prospects of survival.

When Son Muhammad enters to clear the tray of empty dishes, I try to catch his eye, but he looks away. I understand I will have to wait for another opportunity.

As always, Naveh grows tired first and lies down early. It must be a little before 9:00 p.m. now. Adi goes to sit beside him as he falls asleep and speaks with him softly. Naveh shares his thoughts and fears, reliving the horrific scenes he witnessed when the terrorists forced us out of the safe room, our friends' bodies lying near our home in Be'eri, the hate-filled terrorists shoving us at gunpoint toward the car that will whisk us into Gaza. He asks his mother questions: *What will happen to us? Will we die in the airstrikes tonight? When will we get out?* Adi strokes his head, tries to calm and reassure him, and wishes him good night.

I am still on high alert, waiting for a chance to ask Son Muhammad for flatbreads. Then I get my lucky break. The wind seeping through the cracks in the street-facing window blows the curtains aside, threatening to expose us to the neighbors in the building across the square. We are forbidden from approaching the windows, so I motion for him to come and point at the window. He enters, shuts the curtains, and tries to secure them to stop them from billowing again.

When he finishes, we make brief eye contact, and I dare to ask for more flatbread. He leaves the room without answering, but a few minutes later, he returns with a black plastic bag containing two flatbreads. I thank him sincerely and think to myself, *Another small victory in the struggle to survive.*

It is probably already 10:00 p.m. I settle in to sleep beside Naveh, and after us, Noam and Sharon go to sleep as well.

When everyone is already stretched out on their mattresses, Yula stays awake for over an hour and asks to eat. Adi gives her a small piece from one of the new flatbreads. Around us, the airstrikes resume, now terrifyingly close.

We lunge for the foam cushions again in panic to shield the children's heads. By now, they are used to the blasts and just sleep through them. But every time I am torn from sleep, I hum the "Palmach Anthem" in my head, like a mantra. So as not to think. To sleep. In order to live.

Though the storm is ever raging
Still, we raise our sights afar.

We have survived another day in captivity.

How many more?

CHAPTER VII
WILL WE GO BACK?

IN ONE OF MY CONVERSATIONS with Son Muhammad, he asks me, "If you go back, will you go back to the kibbutz?"

If I am released from captivity, will I go back to Kibbutz Be'eri? *If?* I tell him stop saying "if," because we are definitely getting out of here. As for going back to Be'eri, I answer that it is a good question, but I resist sharing my thoughts. I do not want to give him and his comrades the sense that their terror attack achieved its purpose.

Because the truth is that even now, I suspect that I will not return to live in Be'eri. It is painful to imagine being uprooted from the place that was everything to me—the kibbutz my parents founded, where I planted roots both physical and emotional, whose community has been interwoven into my life since the day I was born. But I understand that I cannot go back to living within walking distance of the Gaza Strip. Our brutal abduction, the sight of murdered friends and smoldering homes, the loss of my entire family's freedom, all these have made me grasp, more keenly than I ever dreamed possible, our terrifying proximity to

Gaza and to a people ruled by a terrorist organization whose stated goal is to annihilate us. Even during captivity, I understand that returning to live in the place where this all happened will never allow me to heal from the trauma.

On the day after our kidnapping, and from time to time thereafter, our captors ask whether we have foreign citizenships. Once I answer, "I have to check…" as if I could rummage through my purse or closet at home, to see whether I have a foreign passport. This is a sensitive subject because not all of us have foreign citizenship, but at a certain point I feel I can no longer dodge the question. They could demand an answer at gunpoint at any moment, and the idea of lying fills me with dread: what *if they find out and make us pay a price?* So, the next time they ask, I tell them that Adi, Naveh, Yula, and I have German citizenship. My sister-in-law Sharon and her daughter Noam, however, hold no foreign citizenship at all. It is clear to me they will report this immediately to their commanders.

A few days later, I sit down to talk with Son Muhammad again, and he remarks that the next time they attack us and abduct us again, he cannot guarantee that the team assigned to "handle" us will be so nice. Placing his palm on his chest, he says, "If you go back to Israel, I advise you 'from the heart'"—that's an expression he learned from us in Hebrew—"use your foreign passports and go somewhere else. Abroad. Maybe Europe, or Florida. As far as we're concerned, this time was only a test of our capabilities. We used three thousand Hamas men in the attack, only 10 percent of our forces. Next time, we will strike with full force and conquer the whole country."

"We are going back to Israel," I push back, firmly and forcefully. "And if you say 'if' again, I won't speak with you anymore!" In our later conversations, he is careful to say, "*When* you go back."

I feel he is playing mind games with me. Cruel psychological tricks. He is clearly trying to undermine my faith in our right to live in Kibbutz Be'eri, anywhere near the Gazan border, or for that matter, anywhere in Israel at all.

So I tell him, "*Ana khatyara, ana.*" *I am old, I am.* "Don't talk to me about plans for the future."

"*Inti shababah, inti,*" Son Muhammad replies. *You are young, you are.* I assume he means it as a mark of respect.

The airstrikes and artillery fire around us intensify dramatically, and I ask him whether he is afraid he will be killed. His answer surprises me. With a shrug, he says that he and his comrades are like zombies—alive one day, dead the next. He is indifferent to his own life, married to his mission. And I think of his three "martyred" brothers, surely raised as he was. And I think, too, of the gaping chasm with our own view of life, one sanctifies life itself as the highest value.

***

The hardest days for us are the ones when our captors wake up in the morning and make a point of ignoring us all day, cutting off contact completely. I assume this happens when they have heard radio reports about the Israeli Air Force's overnight strikes, which have dealt Hamas some deadly blows. This cold shoulder, which the children cannot understand, feels deeply threatening.

From time to time, our captors tell us about direct strikes that have affected them personally. Kid Muhammad tells us that his nephew was killed in an airstrike, and that his own house was bombed and destroyed. He had taken out a mortgage to buy that house, he tells us, and that even though it now lies in ruins, he will still have to pay back the mortgage in full.

We struggle to absorb this information because it feels like they are telling us about their problems to make us realize we are on the "wrong side" in this story. Are they trying to get us to defect? Is this another one of their mind games? And yet, I hope that the fact that we are an asset they have been ordered to protect will shield us from any outbursts of anger, revenge, or violence.

As on countless occasions in captivity, I stifle my emotions. I force my mind to focus on other things, lest I sink into depression and lose my strength.

One evening, our captors decide to stage a mock Shin Bet interrogation that will supposedly take place when we return to Israel. This "interrogation" is ostensibly in good humor, but the lighthearted mood is only a wafer-thin veneer over the pervasive knowledge that they have a large stash of weapons next door.

"What will you tell Shin Bet investigators about us?" Son Muhammad asks me.

And I answer, only half in jest, "What can I even tell them? You moved us from apartment to apartment in total darkness. We have no idea where we are. The windows are always covered with curtains. We have no contact with anyone but you. You are all called 'Muhammad,' and you all look the same: skinny, short black hair, trimmed close, and a short little beard."

"And what will you tell Shin Bet about the conditions in captivity?"

And I answer, "The truth. That you guarded us like professionals, fed us three times a day, brought a doctor to treat the children when they got sick, played with the children. I will simply describe reality here."

"Even if you say it's the truth, nobody will believe you," he replies.

***

In my conversations with our captors, I have mixed feelings about the power dynamics between us. Obviously as hostages held at gunpoint, we are the weak and they are the strong ones. But I also know we come from the strong side of the story.

Since independence, the State of Israel has developed advanced capabilities in many fields, including agriculture and industry, and has become one of the world's leading high-tech economies, while also serving as a model, vibrant, and distinctive democracy in the heart of the Middle East. Israel's quality of life, immeasurably higher than in Gaza, stems from its historical choices to focus on building the future, from the days of the first mass Jewish immigration to the absorption of millions of Jews who survived the Holocaust and the Second World War. Israel's success is also a product of its strategic choice to embrace political compromise—the Zionist movement accepted the United Nations Partition Plan of 1947—while at the same time investing in military capabilities to defend ourselves against those who wish to kill us.

By contrast, the people of the Gaza Strip have received billions of dollars in aid from countries and international organizations. From the moment they elected Hamas in 2005 until today, they chose to invest most of their resources in building offensive capabilities in the service of jihad and in pursuit of their goal of annihilating Israel and extending the rule of Islam over the entire planet.

***

Life in Be'eri flashes in front of my eyes in almost every conversation with our captors, including when we talk about economic matters. In one conversation, I am surprised to learn that Gazans use the Israeli shekel. After all, a currency is no mere technical means of payment. It also signals belonging to an economic, cultural, and political system. I admit I have never really looked into the issue, but if you had asked me, I would have guessed they used the Egyptian pound.

In another conversation, Son Muhammad asks me about wages in Israel, then compares them to those in the Gaza Strip, which are of course much lower.

Our captors tell me that a Hamas operative earns about eight hundred shekels a month (around two hundred American dollars), and they ask what the average salary is in Israel. I know the answer; in Be'eri, I was the community's social welfare officer, and many of our calculations were based on the national average monthly wage (around twelve thousand shekels, or fifteen times what he mentions). But I dare not reveal the real sum and throw an estimate of five thousand shekels. Even that is six times their paycheck.

***

Our captors tell us that two of them, Commander Muhammad and Kid Muhammad, are married with children, and that the other two—aged twenty-four and twenty-five—are still unmarried. They explain that their mothers choose their brides for them. The mothers inquire about the women's families and personalities, ultimately deciding whether they are worthy of their sons.

A girl's financial status or academic credentials does not matter, they insist. Only her character. I listen, without letting on that I feel they are putting too fine a gloss on the arrangement. I struggle to believe their mothers do not care about the earning potential and education of their precious sons' prospective brides.

Our captors explain, by contrast, that for a man to be considered a worthy candidate for marriage, he must own a home and earn a respectable living. Only then is he admitted into the pool of eligible bachelors—and this is, of course, a difficult club to enter.

The three younger terrorists studied at universities in the Gaza Strip. Son Muhammad has a bachelor's degree in engineering. Kid Muhammad has a degree in Islamic studies. Nice Muhammad is a qualified accountant. But none of them works in his profession. After finishing college, they enlisted in Hamas.

Commander Muhammad tends to sit out these conversations. We learn that he holds a degree in social work and that his wife is a psychologist. From the moment the abduction unit hands us over to him until the final minutes before our release, he never leaves our side. There are times we find our captors' room empty, but then we hear his voice through the wall and realize he is meeting a visitor. The younger Muhammads, by contrast, go out from time to time to their families and return freshly groomed with a clean change of clothes.

Gaza's youth experience economic hardship in many walks of life. Son Muhammad tells us they do not have passports; some people get to leave the Strip using transit permits. Even getting a driver's license is hard because it costs a prohibitive five thousand dollars. When I ask what the license looks like, he explains that besides the photo, it includes the driver's first name, his father's and grandfather's names, and his clan name. For example: Muhammad, Ahmad, Mahmoud, from the Hamdan clan. I tell him that Ethiopia has a similar system.

When he asks how I know about Ethiopia, I tell him about Fair Planet and its guiding principle of empowering smallholder farmers to exit poverty by providing high-quality seeds and the farming knowledge they need to secure their own future. He immediately asks whether I would also be willing to help farmers in Gaza. First there must be real, stable peace between the Palestinians and Israel, I answer—and then we will gladly come back to help them.

At one point in our conversation, Son Muhammad notes that Gazan workers employed in Israel, when circumstances allow it, earn far more than those on the payroll of Hamas, Islamic Jihad, or UNRWA.

That reminds me of the four Gazans who worked for many years in Be'eri and were considered excellent builders. One of them, Khaled, renovated my parents' home, and they grew very fond of him. My mother had a special connection to Gaza because she studied the city extensively for a geography research project, so she and Khaled had plenty to talk about. Every day, the four laborers ate lunch in Be'eri's bustling communal dining hall and formed friendships with many of our neighbors. We thought that the simple fact that they earned a dignified living with us, providing for their families while befriending ours, would help to foster deeper familiarity between our two peoples and thus lay the groundwork for future coexistence and peace.

But we did not fully understand the ferocity of their frustration as they saw our spacious homes, manicured lawns, and pretty trees and flowers, gaining a glimpse of our comfortable lives. We could not fathom the power of the envy festering in their hearts when, at the end of each workday, they returned to their homes in Gaza—back to neglect, hardship, and widespread unemployment. We foolishly assumed that they would see us as a model and become inspired to build a better future for themselves and their families.

In his novel *The Post-Office Girl*, Stefan Zweig describes the life of a village postal clerk in Austria ravaged by poverty after the First World War. The woman can barely support herself and her sick, elderly mother. One day, her wealthy relatives invite her to join them for a vacation in the Swiss Alps, where she is whisked to cloud nine. She adopts the persona of a wealthy socialite, courted by the young and rich. But when the vacation ends, she is forced to return to her village and impoverished reality. After tasting that glitzy wealth, she can no longer bear to return to dreary squalor. She concludes that such an existence is pointless and turns to violence, throwing her life off course.

Catastrophically for us, we overlooked that crucial lesson.

The situation was even worse. When Gazans were barred from working in Israel in 2007, Kibbutz Be'eri continued paying their salaries for over a year. When the kibbutz decided to stop paying, several members decided to crowdfund for the four workers' families. And as always when kibbutz members fundraise, the kibbutz secretariat matched the amount. For the people of Be'eri, this was a noble act of giving. We failed to grasp that on the Gazan side, this might have been seen as charity for the poor and thus felt humiliating.

I choose not to tell our captors about this. My gut tells me this is not the time or place.

After a while, a chilling thought passes through my mind: The Gazans who worked for us also built our safe rooms. They know every detail of the buildings on the kibbutz—who lived in each house, where their safe rooms were, and how they were laid out, including the location of the door, the strength of the walls, the thickness of the armored door, the structure of their steel-plated windows.

Doubts keep gnawing at me: Did they pass this information to Hamas? Did they supply the terrorists with critical details ahead of the attack on October 7? Did they or did their families, who we fundraised for, join the killing spree?

A few months after we are released, I gather the courage to look up Khaled on WhatsApp. My new phone—the terrorists looted my old one on October 7—has Khaled's number stored, but not our chat history. Gone are the messages in which Khaled asked about my parents' health, then sent condolences after my mother dies, and a year after that, after my father. On the screen, at the top, there is a status update: "Last seen yesterday at 21:18."

Khaled is alive! And he is one WhatsApp message away.

Will I ever dare to contact him?

At this stage, I decide not to. I prefer not to know, so I cling onto the little trust I still hold in the human relationship we forged. Perhaps in the future, when everything that happened that horrific day is investigated in full, the facts will come to light. Even then, I am not sure I will want to know the truth.

***

One of my hardest moments in captivity is when I wake from a dream about two of my grandsons: four-year-old Nahar Shalom and two-year-old Sinai Moshe, the children of my daughter Shaked and her partner, Daniel. In the first few seconds after waking, I still feel their presence beside me. I can practically see their faces, their sweet curls, their blue eyes, and their bubbling laughter. When I snap back to full alertness, I am overcome with suffocating longing.

I remember another dream. We return to Be'eri. I see that the house was hit by the terrorists' bullets. The walls are riddled with holes. We call Rafi, a builder from the southern Israeli Bedouin city of Rahat. He fixes the damage with devotion and love and restores the house to how it used to be.

Meanwhile, in reality, Nice Muhammad asks us one day to teach them Hebrew. We love the idea but impose a condition: They have to teach us Arabic. Once that is agreed, they bring us new notebooks—UNRWA, again—a rare and exciting essential because the kids' old notebooks are already full to bursting. We begin a new routine: One day, we teach our language; the next, we learn theirs.

Adi volunteers to be the Hebrew teacher, and from that moment on, they address her as *muallimah*, teacher, and punctiliously follow her instructions. She teaches them the rules of grammar, final letters, and first-, second-, and third-person conjugations, and gives them assignments for the next lesson.

We do not have a fixed Arabic tutor, by contrast. Usually it is Kid Muhammad, but sometimes two or three of them sit with us (absenting the commander) and help us practice writing and understand the rules of Arabic.

In one conversation, I tell Son Muhammad, "I'll bet you one thing, these children will be the top of their Arabic class back in Israel."

"But in Florida, you won't need to know Arabic," he answers. Trying to mess with our minds again.

The children enjoy the Arabic lessons immensely. They are happy to learn new words and draw the beautiful letters in their notebooks. The terrorists, for their part, enjoy learning Hebrew.

Nice Muhammad turns out to be a star pupil. He carefully writes Hebrew words in his notebook and from time to time, outside their formal lessons, asks Adi the *muallimah* to check his homework.

While our conversations with the terrorists are always conducted in whispers, when they start learning Hebrew, they practice out loud. We panic, fearing the neighbors—or Son Muhammad's little brothers—will hear Hebrew and discover our hiding place. We keep calling them out, but not always with success. They simply cannot get used to whispering, putting us in mortal peril.

***

In our early days in captivity, the terrorists listen to a transistor radio broadcasting news and other programs in Arabic, keeping the volume low. From time to time, we catch a few names in Hebrew and try to figure out what is happening in Israel and the state of the war. But because we hear only random words, the context escapes us. Adi has excellent hearing, and every so often, amid the stream of Arabic that neither of us understands, she says to me, "I think they just said Kiryat Shmona and Jerusalem. Has the war reached there too?" I tell her she cannot infer what is happening from random words. Maybe a rocket hit, or something like that, and that's why the cities were mentioned. But deep down, I entertain a terrifying thought: Is this Israel's second war of independence? Are we under attack on every front again?

About three weeks after we are abducted, our captors' conditions are upgraded when they bring in a television. They turn the screen their way and watch at full blast. The noise spills into our space, even hours after we put the children to bed and try to doze off ourselves. The experience is unbearable, not only because the noise is a nuisance, but because the broadcasts are packed with heated debates and shouting matches that only aggravate our despair.

One evening, the terrorists call Naveh excitedly to come watch the Arabic version of *American Idol* with them. It is rare for any of us to be summoned to their room, but one of the contestants is a child who looks like Naveh, and the terrorists want to make him happy. Naveh joins them willingly, until suddenly he bolts back to us, sobbing uncontrollably. The show was interrupted by a news bulletin showing dead bodies from the war. The footage leaves Naveh shaken for a whole hour. The terrorists come over to him, apologize, and explain that they had no intention of making him watch that graphic footage.

I get the impression they are speaking from the heart.

CHAPTER VIII
UNDERSTANDING

A FEW DAYS AFTER THE television arrives, the captors watch an Al Jazeera report that includes a brief sync in Hebrew. I hear only one sentence—someone screaming, "It happened on your watch!"—but Adi also catches the number 1,400. That's how many were murdered on October 7. She comes over to me straight away, terrified, and says, "Mom, listen—that's 1,400 of *our people*."[4]

Until now, we had no idea of the scale of what happened on October 7. When the terrorists marched us through the kibbutz, we saw and understood that they had conquered Be'eri and that no one was coming to save us, but we had no idea the pogrom would rage for hours, even once we were already in Gaza.

The broadcast Adi happens to overhear is the first time we grasp the magnitude of the horror. We do not even know about the attacks on other communities. So when I hear "1,400," I

4 This was the initial figure reported following the attack. The official death toll was later revised to approximately 1,200 after the complex process of victim identification was finalized.

think perhaps Hamas terrorists eliminated everyone in Be'eri, including the outside visitors, because that is roughly how many people were on the kibbutz for the Simchat Torah holiday.

The news is soul-crushing. We go into total shock.

The next day, I tell Adi and Sharon two things. First, now we understand the scale of the disaster, which means we can brace ourselves mentally for horrific news when we return. Second, it means our time in captivity will not be short, and we must prepare ourselves psychologically for that as well.

It is important for me that this realization sink in for all of us and that we brace ourselves for what it means, because we have been obsessively guessing how long it will take until we are released. We have been basing ourselves on past operations in Gaza, some of which lasted only a few days; the longest, Operation Protective Edge in 2014, lasted fifty days. We used to listen to the Israeli airstrikes, hear the retaliatory rocket fire from the vicinity of the nearby mosque, and sink into the same game of speculation and punditry. But now that we know *1,400 people were killed on October 7,* I understand that this war is a whole different beast. That there is no point trying to predict the dynamics of the war as we experience it from this corner of captivity. I know that if Israel took such a terrible blow, that means a prolonged round of conflict. This knowledge prepares us mentally for a long stretch of captivity.

Until now, I have felt like a mountain hiker braving an untrodden path. Every pause of a few hours in the bombardments feels like a sign that we are about to reach the summit and can then finally begin descending toward our release, toward home. And every time the hostilities kick off again, I feel the tumbling disappointment. It is like another menacing peak has materialized in front of me, one I must climb all over again. But now it is clear: The road to freedom will be long and grueling, far more so than I have been banking on.

I decide to stop being a pundit. There is no point trying to guess whether a ceasefire and hostage deal is imminent or not. We must breathe deeply and muster every fiber of strength in order not to break. We must hang in there.

I swallow my emotions and tell Adi and Sharon, "In any case, we'll be the first ones out of here. With all the women and children, or with all the civilians. Because Hamas' interest is for Israel to free their prisoners. And if the women and children aren't released safely, Israel won't give them anything."

***

After some time, who knows how long, I hear heavy artillery and then detect that the IDF has launched its ground offensive into the Gaza Strip. How can I describe it? The only metaphor that comes to mind is chariots of fire. A mighty military force starts rolling in under nonstop gunfire, bringing fire and clamor on an epic scale.

In my imagination, I see what is happening. I hear this aggressive development and understand, beyond doubt, that the negotiations between Israel and Hamas over our release have reached a dead end. Our side is bringing new cards to the table. It is trying to create a new form of pressure. I get the sense that our captors did not believe this moment would actually come, that the IDF would launch a ground offensive into Gaza. But this, of course, we leave unspoken.

In any case, I understand that with the ground operation, the IDF is shifting gears to destroying Hamas' tunnels. This realization is also based on hearing, the only sense connecting us to the outside world, but it is obvious. I hear two weak blasts, followed by an almighty explosion. Again and again.

At this point, we are close to getting out, but of course, we do not know it yet.

I did not know at the time that a comprehensive NATO report, published as early as 2019, had already documented the very tactics I was witnessing in captivity.[5] The report confirms that Hamas uses "human shields" by firing rockets from within densely populated areas and employs "religious shields" by operating from mosque courtyards. While I could hear that rockets were being launched from the nearby mosque, the report provided chilling evidence of tactics hidden from my view: the systematic exploitation of schools, hospitals, and clinics, and even the use of ambulances to transport both terrorists and weaponry.

And even now as I write these lines, I've read about the many institutions that knew about Hamas' deliberate use of civilians as human shields, including the United Nations, the European Union, the United States, and Israel. I am stunned to learn that over the years, Hamas has even explicitly said that it saw Palestinian civilian casualties as not only unavoidable, but as something that advanced its mission.[6]

It is clear to me that Hamas is deliberately hiding us, the hostages, in the heart of a civilian neighborhood in order to shield its terrorists with our own bodies, but only after I get out does it dawn on me that for Hamas, Palestinian civilians serve the same purpose. They are a means to tarnish Israel's image.

---

5 James Pamment et al., *Hybrid Threats: Hamas' Use of Human Shields in Gaza* (NATO Strategic Communications Centre of Excellence, 2019).

6 Summer Said and Rory Jones, *Gaza Chief's Brutal Calculation: Civilian Bloodshed Will Help Hamas (Wall Street* Journal, June 10, 2024)

Hamas inflicts its cynicism, malice, and cruelty on its own people, its own flesh and blood. For Hamas, everything is permitted in service of the supreme goal of jihad, the conquest and annihilation of the State of Israel, and the imposition of Islamic rule over the world.

***

About six weeks after our abduction, Kid Muhammad approaches me and asks me to write our shoe sizes on a tiny slip of paper. This is the first hint that we are getting out soon—in Gaza, people remove their shoes before entering a home and walk around barefoot inside. Shoes, therefore, symbolize leaving the house.

We do not have shoes because we were kidnapped barefoot. When they moved us between hideouts, the terrorists gave us secondhand flip-flops. I ask Adi and Sharon for their shoe sizes and the children's. When I hand the terrorist the slip of paper with the details, he says we will get the shoes tomorrow.

With enormous excitement, I tell the women what I think this means.

Some hours later, Son Muhammad brings a scale to weigh the children. I assume the mediators or negotiators have demanded specific, verifiable data—details more biological and less administrative than just names and ages. It occurs to me that by providing the children's current weights, Hamas is offering a "proof of life" update. These figures may give the negotiators more certainty that the children are indeed in their custody. As it happens, they exempt us mothers from being weighed.

Son Muhammad jots down the numbers: Yula weighs just under thirty pounds; Naveh, sixty-eight pounds. I do not manage to see Noam's weight, but the fact that they are weighing the children tells me that they are preparing to release us.

We choose not to share our optimism with the children, to spare them the possibility of disappointment. Still, I am so hopeful I could fly. It is hard to describe how my heartbeat is racing, how adrenaline is flooding my body, how I fight to temper my anticipation.

But the next day, nothing happens. The terrorists do not bring us shoes; they do not even speak with us. Disappointment and despair hit us hard.

And once again, we hear hostilities erupting around the house, but we are completely cut off, clueless about what is happening or what lies ahead.

A few more days nerve-racking pass, until a relatively steady quiet returns. One morning, Kid Muhammad approaches me and again asks for everyone's shoe sizes. I realize he must have destroyed my earlier note; they were fanatical about hiding any trace of our presence in the house, maintaining a strict policy of destroying all paperwork. He says he will bring the shoes the next day so we can try them on, adding that he will swap the sizes if needed.

And this time, it really happens. Kid Muhammad arrives with a pile of brand-new shoe boxes, and we open them eagerly. Even in captivity, new gifts are a joy.

But even now, we decide not to share with the children our hope that this means we are about to get out. We still fear another letdown.

For us, the mothers, Muhammad brings black suede moccasins, with diamond-like embellishments at the front, and black lace socks. For Naveh, he brings shiny black leather dress shoes. For Yula, tiny sneakers with pink decorations. And for Noam, white sneakers with a black Nike logo. Naveh is disappointed with his pair and wants the same as Noam; mine are too small and pinch my toes.

Kid Muhammad keeps his promise. Not only does he agree to exchange my size, but he also grants Naveh's request, and about two hours later, the replacement shoes arrive. As we try them on, Kid Muhammad tells us that his wife just had a baby and he bought us these shoes as a gift, out of pocket, as part of the celebrations around the expansion of his family.

Our excitement swells again. We understand that negotiations for our release are underway and that the date is drawing near. *Maybe this time it will really happen....*

A few more days pass with no more echoes of war. The cease-fire seems to be holding this time. We notice that the drones, which were always buzzing overhead, are gone. I infer the IDF has stopped gathering intelligence about events on the ground in Gaza. An unusual quiet descends around us. Perhaps this is another sign that we're about to get out of here.

One morning, Adi notices that a stranger has arrived to meet our band of captors, and they forget to close the partition. She steps back immediately, to avoid accidentally making eye contact, but then the terrorists enter our room with him.

The man asks her name.

"Adi Shoham," she replies.

Then he tells her that he is her husband Tal's guard, and says, in English, "He is fine, he is healthy, he is completely OK." And when he spots Naveh, he says, "How he looks like his father! Tal tells me so much about you. He misses you and the children." And we begin to believe he is telling the truth.

Immediately, our captors burst into cries of "*Mabrouk, mabrouk, mabrouk*!" We burst into tears of joy and excitement.

In the most horrifically absurd way, their happiness seems genuine. They are happy for us.

The man tells Adi that he has been on Tal's guarding squad for several weeks, that they talk a lot, and that they have formed a solid connection.

Then he asks her, "Do you have a younger sister?"

"Yes," she answers.

"Is her husband Daniel?"

"Yes."

"Is his family from Iran?"

"Yes."

Now we are sure: This man really is Tal's guard. Only someone who spoke with him personally could know all those details. It's not like there is a paper trail.

Excitement beyond measure washes over us.

Meanwhile, the terrorists huddle in their room for a long conversation. From the dynamic between them, we conclude they already know each other; this stranger is their friend. After some time, they ask Adi whether she wants to send Tal a letter for his guard to deliver. After some hesitation, she decides to write a short letter in English and hands it to the guard, who promises it will reach the addressee.

I muster the courage to ask whether they know anything about what happened to Avshal. They say they have no idea. I believe them. I have already assumed that Hamas enforces strict compartmentalization among the guard squads, and that information flows only upward, to their commanders.

I have a hunch that the reason the stranger came to visit—and did not hide from us—is that they already know the ceasefire has entered into force ahead of a deal that will see us released in exchange for their prisoners. That, I think, is why their discipline around compartmentalization and secrecy has begun to slip.

The daylight hours pass while we are still overwhelmed with emotion, trying to stay composed to spare ourselves the crushing disappointment, if it comes.

The next evening, the terrorists ask us to gather for a meeting, together with the children. They tell us that the process of our release will probably begin the following morning at the break of dawn. They put the odds at 70 percent, but we need to get ready anyway.

Then they explain to the children that, for the first time since they were assigned to guard us, they will be armed and wearing Hamas uniforms and face masks. But they ask them to remember that they are still friends, and they will protect them, just as they have protected them all along.

A few minutes later, Son Muhammad tells the children, "Hang on, let's put on what we're going to wear tomorrow, and we'll come show you so you won't be afraid." And indeed, he and Nice Muhammad step out and return wearing mottled Hamas uniforms, holding black face masks and green headbands. They sit down beside the children and demonstrate how they put on the face masks, covering their whole faces except their eyes, and tie their green Hamas headbands across their foreheads. "Tomorrow, listen to our voices," they tell the children, "then you will know it is us, your friends."

Son Muhammad explains the process: We will be moved through several houses before being handed over to the Red Cross, who will transfer us through Egypt to Israel. He adds that we will be allowed to leave with only the clothes on our backs and shoes on our feet. Later that evening, they will bring women to conduct a body search and make sure we are not smuggling any contraband. Then he asks us to go sleep that night in the clothes we will wear on the road to freedom.

With immense excitement, we begin settling down for the last night before we get out of here. Adi puts on a leopard-print shirt and black pants, helping Yula into pink pajamas with little crescent-moon patterns. Naveh dresses himself, throwing on a blue sweatshirt and dark pants. Sharon puts on a dark burgundy dress, and Noam gets into Mickey Mouse pajamas.

I put on a thick sweatshirt because I do not want to be cold, but the terrorists ask me to change into something more "presentable." It matters to them that we look "respectable" during the release. I switch into a burgundy tunic with white Bedouin embroidery, slipping my mother's shawl, the same one I was wearing when they pulled me out of the safe room on that horrific October 7, into a small pocket.

These are the clothes in which we will later be photographed in hundreds of pictures and video clips covering our release, clothes that none of us would willingly choose to wear in any other situation.

They scoop up all our other clothes, along with the notebooks with our drawings and Arabic studies. The same goes for the toys, after the children say goodbye to Fufu, the blue Smurf with the red hat, who has kept them company them for fifty days. Huli, the Papa Smurf with the yellow hat, has already disappeared, and our attempts to find him a few days earlier have left us empty handed. We turned our room upside down and asked the terrorists to look in theirs because the children were truly heartbroken, but to no avail.

Suddenly, the terrorists call Adi over to watch a live broadcast on television. On the screen, live, a group of hostages is walking free—on the first day of the deal—after forty-nine days in captivity. The group includes nine women and four small children, most of them abducted from Kibbutz Nir Oz.

Adi watches. She cannot make out the identity of the released hostages but discovers in horror that as they are handed to the Red Cross, they are surrounded by hundreds of Gazans, forming a rowdy and threatening mob around them. Son Muhammad tells her to expect an angry crowd at our release too, but that we have nothing to fear, because they are all Hamas people who will obey their commanders' orders. The shouting is just for show.

Later, two young women arrive in black burqas, with only their eyes poking through a narrow slit. They frisk us, then we go to sleep. We lie beside the children, who fall asleep as usual, but we cannot close our eyes. The adrenaline, the thoughts, and the hopes are making our heads spin.

All night, we wait for dawn.

And then morning comes, and nothing happens. I look at Adi, and despair seeps into our hearts. About an hour later, Commander Muhammad walks in and says he is still waiting for the green light to release us; he does not know if or when it will come. Exhausted from the tension and uncertainty, we fall asleep again. About four hours later, our captors wake us.

"It's approved," they say. "Quickly, get ready."

CHAPTER IX
THE ROAD TO FREEDOM

ALL FOUR OF OUR CAPTORS are now dressed in Hamas uniforms, with black face masks and green headbands. Each of them is strapped into an ammunition belt carrying grenades and bullets. It is as if simply putting on their uniforms makes them stand up taller and boosts their self-esteem. They look proud, confident, and mission-driven. Warriors in the service of jihad to destroy the State of Israel. That is their raison d'être.

Yet, in complete contrast to their threatening exterior, they make a point of approaching the children gently and reminding them not to be afraid of them.

Abdullah from next door, also wearing a mottled uniform and tactical vest, joins them and accompanies us for the release process. Only now do I understand that he was not some nosy neighbor that they were forced to put up with occasionally and keep away from us, but a Hamas operative just like them.

Kid Muhammad notices the bulge in my pants pocket and asks what it is. I show him the shawl and explain that I received it from my mother and that it has sentimental value. He agrees that I can keep it. In these moments, I have no idea that the terrorists blew up my house, obliterating everything inside it. This shawl is the only thing I have left from my mother.

At around 10:00 a.m., the terrorists announce that we are heading out and instruct us, the women, to cover up in hijabs. They station themselves around us, two in front and two behind, and together, we walk downstairs to the ground floor. Outside the house, in a covered parking lot, is a waiting vehicle. Two terrorists get in up front, and we squeeze into the back, in the same formation as when we were abducted: Naveh on my lap, Yula on Adi's, and Noam on Sharon's.

There is another car waiting outside the yard and I notice that Abdullah is already in it. The two other captors step inside and join him. The two cars start their engines, pass the square that serves as a parking area for buses and ambulances, pass the shopping center, and continue driving through alleyways. Every so often, we see the hull of a bombed-out building at the side of the road, and the terrorists make a point of telling us that we are looking at the aftermath of Israeli airstrikes.

There are almost no other cars in the alleyways, ostensibly because of a fuel shortage in Gaza, although Hamas' vehicles are well fueled. I notice people walking on the streets, their faces blank and indifferent. Some are carrying yellow water jerricans on their backs; the lucky ones are leading donkeys that are carrying the jerricans for them. I am reminded of similar scenes I have seen in the poorest parts of Ethiopia when I've done humanitarian work with Fair Planet.

From time to time, passersby ogle at us curiously through the car windows, but we look straight ahead and hope that the hijabs will stop them from figuring out who we are. All of us are silent.

After a while, we pass another destroyed building, and Son Muhammad points at it and says that it is Kid Muhammad's house, the one for which he will continue having to pay the mortgage, even though it no longer exists.

The car ahead stops in an alleyway. The three terrorists get out, apparently to confer, and we remain in the rear car with our two captors. These minutes of waiting feel like an eternity. The terrorists return to their car, and we continue until we reach a main road. From the position of the sun, I realize we are traveling south.

After about twenty minutes, we turn left onto a narrow side road and stop beside a building surrounded by a fenced yard with an iron gate. We roll into the yard and wait in the vehicle. One of the terrorists steps out for another consultation, returns, and off we go again. After two more similar stops, we reach the house that will be our final holding place in Gaza before our release.

The terrorists lead us through a narrow corridor into a large room with three velvet couches, a small table in the center, and several chairs. To the right of the corridor is a bathroom, this time with running water. After we settle down, they bring in a huge tarpaulin banner printed with Arabic text and illustrations of jihad. They tape it to the wall and ask us to stand in front of it with the children for a group photograph with them. The photo is taken while they are, of course, still kitted out in full Hamas combat gear.

About an hour later, a woman enters the room wrapped in a light, floral hijab, wearing slanted glasses, and holding the hand of a teenage girl. I look at them; the woman looks familiar. Before I work out who she is, she calls out my name, removes the fake glasses the terrorists made her wear, and yanks off her hijab. I recognize her at once: It's Shiri Weiss, from my kibbutz, with her eighteen-year-old daughter Noga.

In the first second, I feel embarrassed that I did not recognize her immediately. Clearly a holdover from my previous life, before the catastrophe that sliced my life in two, when you meet someone you know you know but cannot remember their name. But then, as soon as I snap back, the penny drops. *More people from Be'eri were kidnapped to Gaza.* We were not the only ones.

We share a long, tight embrace. Our experiences in captivity have been complicated and traumatic, and we struggle to put them into words. After the excitement subsides a little, Shiri tells me that on October 7, she and Noga were home alone when the terrorists broke in. Her husband, Ilan Weiss, a member of Be'eri's emergency response team, went out to fight the terrorists as soon as the news of their invasion arrived. She does not know what happened to him. They learned about the horrific situation from WhatsApp chats with friends. Neighbors wrote that their houses were on fire; then they stopped answering.

In time, we will discover that Ilan was murdered that day near the fence of the kibbutz, and his body was abducted into Gaza. He will only be returned and laid to rest in Be'eri two years later, in September 2025.

"When the terrorists broke into our house," Noga recalls, "Mom told me to go under the bed. She thought they would shoot her on the spot and leave. I hid under the bed, then they came and kidnapped her. I saw everything. Then I heard gunfire outside. I was sure they murdered her. After that, they set the house on fire and I couldn't breathe. My older sister, Meital, WhatsApped me to tell me to escape through the safe room window and hide."

Noga ran to hide, but one of the terrorists noticed her and dragged her into the neighbors' yard, where dozens of armed terrorists swarmed around her. She was cuffed and shoved into a car that stole her into the Gaza Strip. When they crossed the border, she saw thousands of people, including children, whooping and hailing the kidnappers.

Noga was held in captivity with another hostage. One day, Hamas moved her to another house, where she was shocked to see her mother. Until then, she was sure the terrorists had murdered her on October 7. She says that during captivity, one of the terrorists told her he wanted to marry her. "I'm the one who insisted they reunite you two," he said, "so your mother would give permission for the wedding."

Soon, another group of terrorists arrives with more hostages, and I see two more teenagers who were abducted from Be'eri: Noam Or, sixteen, and his thirteen-year-old sister, Alma. We hug. Noam is staggeringly tall, and his thick fringe nearly covers his eyes. Alma is thin and willowy, her brown hair falling over her shoulders. They speak little and say only that they were together most of the time. I sense they have neither the capacity nor the desire to share any more, and I offer only emotional support.

I notice that our four captors and Abdullah are the most senior of all the terrorists who begin to assemble at this holding house. They are the ones issuing orders to the others and managing the entire event. Commander Muhammad sits in the main office behind a large desk, exchanging occasional words on a landline with his own superiors.

After a while, two very young hostages enter the room. I recognize them: Hila Rotem, thirteen, and nine-year-old Emily Hand, also from Be'eri. Hila has a sweet face, with long and wavy brown hair, and tiny Emily—so small, so fragile—has a pale and doll-like complexion. I go over and hug them, and they tell me their story. Little Emily went to stay over at Hila's house on the eve of Simchat Torah, and they were abducted together with Hila's mother, Raaya.

I ask Hila where her mother is. "We were together the whole time in captivity," she says. "A few days ago, the terrorists told us that we're getting released, but Hamas broke the agreement. In the morning, they told us to shower and get ready, but then I saw they weren't getting my mom ready to leave. Mom understood something was off because they hadn't told her anything. And in the evening, they told me and Emily, 'Come, you're going,' and they told my mom, 'You're staying here.'"

The cruelty of separating a mother from her daughter and sending a young teenager and a little girl out alone hits me. In all our time in captivity, it never once occurred to me that our captors might separate us at the moment of our release. And yet here they did it, with such incredible hard-heartedness.

Son Muhammad explains that the plan is to deliver us to the Red Cross, apparently at around 4:00 p.m., and that the handover location is about a twenty-minute drive from the house where we are currently waiting.

Sometime later, he comes over and calls me into the small office room. There, a terrorist I have not seen before—a very fat man whose buttons barely close his Hamas uniform over his swollen belly—is fussing with a tripod and video equipment. Beside him stands another terrorist, this one thin—his assistant. Both are armed, wearing vests and crossed ammunition belts over their chests, and they dictate messages I am to say to Benjamin Netanyahu, the government, and the Israeli people. It is obvious that anyone who watches the video will understand it was filmed under duress at gunpoint and that my words therefore carry no meaning.

They record me reciting their script. Then they ask me to call Shiri and Noga, who must go through the same routine, followed by Noam and Alma Or.

Last to enter the makeshift studio are Hila and Emily. The terrorists ask me to translate the instructions for them. I oblige but slightly alter the messages as I see fit (the cameraman and his assistant do not speak Hebrew; their English is clunky). I string together some lines for Hila. She reads them to the camera.

For little Emily I suggest one simple sentence: "I call on all the citizens of Israel to take to the streets and demonstrate for the release of all the hostages." The cameraman gestures for her to begin, and she recites the words in a trembling, faint voice. He watches it back, decides it is unsatisfactory, and tells me to explain to Emily that she needs to film another take. I see her distress and snap at him, "Enough. Stop. Please don't film again. The little girl's terrified."

He looks at me, hesitates for a moment, and finally says, "OK, Sausan. Go, go, go."

And I think to myself how absurd it is that these terrorists, whom I met only about an hour ago, granted my request, even though they are armed from head to toe, and I am here in nothing but a Bedouin-embroidered red dress.

Time crawls by, and we try to keep the excited children occupied as they wait for our release. Suddenly, I am called again to the office, where I see four terrified Thai men sitting pressed together. Son Muhammad explains that they, too, are marked for release, but the terrorists can barely communicate with them, so he asks me to help translate again.

One of the Thai men turns to me, visibly excited, and tells me in Hebrew that his name is Anucha Angkaew, that he worked on Kibbutz Re'im, and that he was abducted from there with other Thai farmhands. In the first four days, they were chained in the basement of an abandoned house, after which they were held in very harsh conditions in tunnels underground. They do not know why they were taken hostage. Today, to their surprise, the terrorists covered their faces and led them through a tunnel for about two hours until they arrived here.

I explain to Anucha that they will be released together with us and that they have nothing to fear: We are all one group. He relays the information to his friends and it seems to reassure them a little. They thank me with gestures and broken Hebrew.

I return to the large room with the Israeli hostages. The atmosphere is extremely tense, and time passes slowly as we wait for our long-awaited release.

After a while, the film crew enters. The fat man and his slender assistant set up their equipment, install a lighting stand with a powerful lamp, and call over Nice Muhammad. When he comes in, they film him holding a bundle wrapped in layers of white tissue paper. He approaches us and unwraps the bundle until he reaches a smaller package wrapped in aluminum foil. He opens the silver wrapping and presents us the jewelry they stole from us on the day we were kidnapped. We are asked to identify the pieces and take what belongs to us.

Adi recognizes her gold earring. Sharon identifies her delicate gold necklace. Noam spots the colorful fabric bracelets the terrorists took from her in the car. My wedding ring—braided with three types of gold—is not there.

The fat man and the thin assistant film the "return" of the jewelry so the footage can serve Hamas' narrative about "noble

Islamic values." And I think to myself, *Despicable murderers, busy spreading propaganda and lies...*

I ask Nice Muhammad where my ring is, and he asks whether I remember what the terrorist who confiscated it from me looked like. Adi and I describe him in detail, and he says he will check whether the ring is still with him.

Of course, I know it is all a show for propaganda, but I cannot help but entertain the next dilemma: Do I tell them about my diamond-and-sapphire ring, that precious family heirloom? Do I reveal where I hid it in the first house they took us to? My mind is dizzy with thoughts. We are on the brink of walking free. After we are released, I will never get to speak with them again. Maybe they have some shred of integrity after all. Maybe they want to impress me, or themselves. In captivity, we had many conversations about Islam, and they tried to convince us that they have values too. And what do I have to lose? If I say nothing, the ring disappears forever. If I tell them, there is at least a chance, however slim, that we will be reunited.

Time is of the essence. I must decide quickly.

I call Son Muhammad and tell him the story: how I hid the ring, where I buried it, what it looks like. He immediately calls Kid Muhammad, who now, decked in Hamas uniform and armed to the teeth, no longer looks like a kid anymore. He listens to the details and tells me, "I know exactly where the ring is. That's my house. I told you Israel bombed it. But I promise you I will look. If we find the ring, we will return it to you with Tal when he is released."

I notice it immediately. He doesn't say "if." He uses the word I demanded: *when*. Even here, towering over me in his combat fatigues, only his eyes visible through his black face-mask, the linguistic boundary I set holds firm. My ring might not make it home. But Tal *will* come back. I smile wryly.

His words fill me with a certain optimism, but even though this special ring has sentimental value, in these moments, what matters to me above all else is that Tal and the other hostages, like us, finally walk free.

***

At around 4:00 p.m., Son Muhammad approaches us and says, "I am so sorry, I am so sorry." *Something has gone wrong*. He tells us that there is no green light to release us because "Bibi Netanyahu is making new demands that are not in the agreement, so we might have to take you back to the hideouts where you were before." Our spirits collapse. The enormous tension of this long day, its twists and turns, the emotional turmoil of meeting the other hostages, it has all been exhausting and maddening. But I refuse to let myself fall apart.

It is clear to me that this release process—carried out in stages (we watched the first group leave yesterday, and our captors say there will be more after us)—is the result of complex negotiations between Israel and Hamas, probably with the involvement of international actors. I know we are a twenty-minute drive from the Red Cross representatives waiting to receive us. I refuse to believe these negotiations will collapse after 95 percent of the convoluted process of concentrating all the hostages at the final rendezvous is done. I assume one side is applying pressure to extract some additional concessions and that in the end, we will not be dragged back into hell.

I go to each of the hostage groups—Adi, Sharon, and the children; Shiri and Noga; Noam and Alma; Hila and Emily; the four Thai men—and tell them one by one, "We're getting out of here. The crisis will be solved in the coming hours, tomorrow at the latest."

A few minutes later, a young, tall woman enters the building, with sleek black hair and delicate, beautiful features. She limps toward us, leaning on crutches. Her left leg is in a cast reinforced with external iron bars. A Hamas operative who arrives with her joins the terrorists huddling in the office.

I approach her and she tells me her name is Maya Regev. She was waiting in the car outside for about two hours with her "chaperone" because they thought the release process was about to begin, and it was easier for her to sit there, keeping her leg in the cast raised. But when they learned of the delay, they decided to come in despite the difficulty of walking on her injured leg.

Maya asks me to accompany her to the bathroom and support her so she does not slip and fall. Then we return to the room with everyone, and I help her stretch out on the longest sofa. She is so beautiful, and the first thing I ask her is, "Tell me, has anyone already told you how beautiful you are?" I know it is a stupid question, but I see how much agony she is in, and I want to warm her heart. She responds with a shy, slightly bashful smile.

Maya, aged twenty-one, tells me that on October 6, she and her younger brother Itay, eighteen, flew back from a family trip to Mexico. They managed to spend a few hours at their home in Herzliya, before heading out to a nature party in a grove near Kibbutz Re'im, known as the Nova Festival. At 06:29 a.m. on Saturday, all hell broke loose around them as dozens of terrorists raided about four thousand partygoers and started massacring them. The siblings tried to flee, but Maya was shot in her left leg; Itay was shot in both. Then, they were both abducted with their friend Omer Shem Tov. When they crossed into Gaza, the terrorists forced her to walk hundreds of yards through tunnels on her injured leg.

In her first days of captivity, Maya was held with the bullet still lodged in her leg, and the terrorists deliberately hurt her as they changed her bandages. At first, she was held in the same room as Itay and Omer, but they were soon separated. She was moved to another room and saw them only for a few minutes from time to time.

Five days after she was abducted, the terrorists led her through a concrete tunnel dug directly under a hospital. From the shaft, they emerged straight into the hospital. She spent forty-five days in a small room in the hospital, alone with a terrorist guard, except for one instance when she met Guy Illouz, a musician who was also abducted from the Nova festival. Guy, who was shot during his abduction, did not survive his injuries and died by Maya's side about eight days after his kidnapping.

Maya says she suffered physical and psychological abuse in the hospital. Sometimes her doctor poured chlorine, alcohol, or vinegar into her gunshot wounds and pressed on them. To stop her screaming, they drugged her with ketamine and pethidine, which relaxed her muscles but did not relieve her agony. After the doctor extracted the bullet from her leg, he deliberately set the bone at a twisted angle to cause a permanent deformity and increase her suffering.

The terrorists also frightened her constantly. They told her the IDF was killing hostages together with terrorists and taunted her that any rescue attempt by the army would pose a real threat to their lives. "That was my biggest fear," she says, "that someone would come and try to save me in some operation."

I listen to this wonderful young woman at length and hear her describe in detail what she endured in the fifty days since she was shot and abducted from the Nova Festival. Every few minutes, she stops talking to reposition her maliciously reset leg, and her beautiful face contorts with severe pain.

As she speaks, I am struck by the realization that other hostages genuinely went through hell: degrading conditions, sadistic physical abuse, forced isolation, cruel psychological manipulation, and even moments when they were forced to witness their friends dying in agony.

After the announcement of the delay, the terrorists, more than ten of them now, roam between the rooms, armed and in full uniforms, face masks covering their faces. Some gradually become less cautious and remove their masks.

From the behavior of our team of Muhammads, who are running the event, they were clearly not anticipating the delay and were not prepared to keep seventeen hostages in this house overnight. In any case, Naveh, Yula, and Noam, who know them well, seem relatively calm. They trust them.

Night falls, and there is a frantic effort to arrange sleeping options. The terrorists bring mattresses, apparently from neighbors in the area, and consult with me about where to place each hostage. In the small room to the right of the corridor, empty of furniture, we lay out four mattresses for Shiri Weiss, Noga, Hila, and Emily. The four Thai men settle into the small office next to the entrance to the house. I enter the main office, where Commander Muhammad is sitting and speaking on the phone, to see whether we can squeeze any mattresses here as well, but he panics at the fact that I just walked in and gestures for me to scram.

There is no alternative: We have to house nine people in the large room. Son Muhammad and I decide to assign the longest couch to Maya because she must keep her leg straight in the cast. Noam Or and Alma, both tall, are given the other two long couches. For Sharon and Noam, we create a kind of double sleeping bay from two shorter couches by pushing their seats together facing each other.

After we find arrangements for everyone, there is no room left for us. A glance at the living room floor shows it is covered in sand and broken glass. Adi asks Son Muhammad to bring brooms, and we sweep the remaining open area at the far end, lay out three mattresses side by side on the floor, and settle down for sleep. Despite the intense tension, exhaustion overpowers me, and at last I fall asleep next to Naveh, listening to Adi and Yula whispering on my right as they lie by my side.

PART 2
HEALING AND REMEMBRANCE

CHAPTER X
THE RELEASE

ABOUT TWO HOURS LATER, THE terrorists wake us. The green light for our release has come through. We are told to get ready for a hasty departure.

It is pitch black outside. The terrorists usher us into cars waiting in the yard, and once again we sit in the back seat: Naveh on my lap, Yula on Adi's, and Noam on Sharon's, just as when we were taken into Gaza, except now, we are on our way home. The bottomless terror we've felt since then gives way to immense joy, mixed with tension and hope that everything will pass safely.

Six cars carrying excited hostages, escorted by armed terrorists, form a motorcade toward the meeting point with the Red Cross. We are bracing for a violent outburst of rage, the same terrifying ordeal the group of hostages from Nir Oz faced the day before, but our six-hour delay has pushed the release into the dead of night. By midnight, the angry crowds have dispersed, leaving the streets hauntingly empty. The chaos we feared never materializes.

As we approach the rendezvous, one car pulls ahead while the others wait some 450 feet behind. The handover to the Red Cross, step by step, is a slow and cautious process. We are the fourth car in line, and while we wait, Son Muhammad turns around from the front and says, "Naveh, you're so cute. Why do you want to leave? Maybe stay here with us?" I think to myself, *What a bizarre and absurd scene this is....* And yet, I believe that our captors and the children have formed a genuine emotional bond.

After minutes that feel like an eternity, our car begins to move and reaches the rendezvous. The terrorists get out and lead us in pairs, walking alongside us. At the handover point, the children wave goodbye to the Muhammads, who wave back at them.

And then freedom.

Robina and Emilio, an Italian duo, speak with us briefly in English. He has kind eyes, and she has a broad smile. They help us climb into a white Jeep with the Red Cross emblem and the agency's flag flying overhead. Only there, inside the Jeep, do we finally understand: *This is it.* We are returning to the free world.

It is already close to midnight. A convoy of five white Jeeps and one ambulance, brought for Maya with her injury, sets off toward the Rafah crossing between the Gaza Strip and Egypt, carrying seventeen hostages. Seventeen thumping hearts. We barely speak to one another. We are all absorbed in our own inner emotions, frozen in anticipation.

As we approach the border crossing, we see clusters of cars parked on both sides of the dark road, with people crouching around small bonfires. I assume these are Gazans waiting for the rare permits to cross the border into Egypt.

Without any papers and with only the clothes on our backs, we are asked to get out of the Jeeps and enter an office building adjacent to the border, still on Gazan soil. Without inspection or questions, we cross the border and enter Egypt.

Across the border, a coach is waiting to take us to Israel. After we sit down, we hear a voice in Hebrew coming from the loudspeaker system that tour guides usually use. It is an IDF officer congratulating us on our release and explaining that in about twenty minutes, we will reach the Kerem Shalom crossing. Although we are still in a foreign land, hearing Hebrew spoken by a fellow Israeli, who is bringing us under protection, moves us all to tears.

The passage from Egypt into Israel is orderly, and we cross the border swiftly.

We have arrived home.

Dozens of IDF soldiers and officers stand near the gate of the IDF base at Kerem Shalom. They're dressed in neat, clean uniforms, weapons slung properly over their shoulders, ranks on their shoulders. Casualty officers, Spokesperson's Unit representatives, photographers, logistics personnel, guards, and so many more.

When we step off the coach, each of us is assigned a casualty officer. They introduce themselves and escort us to a massive field tent erected to receive returning hostages. The encounter is deeply moving. They greet us warmly and accompany us to the entrance, Naveh holding my hand and Yula wrapped around Adi's waist. At last, I see Adi radiant and happy as she hugs Yula to her chest, both laughing with uninhibited joy. Naveh pulls away from me and runs ahead, a blissful free spirit, into the tent bathed in warm light.

Inside the marquee are play areas for the children, with board games and coloring books laid out on small tables. Beside them, plush teddy bears in an array of colors, surrounded by huge, soft pillows scattered all around.

On the right, in the marquee, are tables stacked with piles of new clothes, sorted by size for children, teenagers, and adults, ready for us to pick something comfortable to replace the outfits we received from the terrorists. On the last table, in the far corner, lie stacks of cozy blankets in warm pastel colors, and in another section are tables laden with pastries, vegetables and fruit, juices, coffee, and an assortment of teas.

My gaze drifts toward Adi, watching in wonder as the children are showered with love, hugging the teddy bears they were just given. I think about the sharp contrast between the army's absence, the abandonment and neglect we experienced on October 7, and the meticulous welcome it has prepared for us now, with soft teddy bears, coloring books, clothes, and refreshments.

Where was the IDF when we truly needed its protection?

Perhaps returning to freedom has allowed me to escape the survival mode I was in during captivity, when my entire being was focused on making the right decisions for each moment. Only now can I articulate, at least to myself, a voice of criticism, without the fear of death that menaced us in the hell of Gaza.

After a while, I ask my casualty officer where the restroom is. She takes me around the back of the tent to the luxury portable toilets, like at an outdoor wedding. On the shelf above the sink is an array of feminine hygiene products, alongside makeup and blush. *They've thought of everything.*

And again, the thought gnaws at me: This is not what we need from the Israel Defense Forces. Not at all. The army was supposed to protect us from the enemy! To guard the border, to prevent the invasion of our communities, the murdering, the kidnapping, the looting, the devastating carnage. In our own sovereign state, with one of the mightiest armies in the world, we suffered a pogrom. Like the pogrom my mother's family endured in Russia 120 years ago. We were abandoned in the face of hundreds of rageful armed terrorists who waltzed across the border and invaded our homes. And no one came to protect us.

I do not share these thoughts with the officer. Instinctively, I know this is neither the time nor the place. The officer, devoted to her role, invites me to share my feelings, to unload my grief and let it all out. I cannot. "If I start talking about all the pain bottled up inside me," I tell her, "if I open even a tiny crack in the thick skin I've built, I will completely fall apart and melt into a puddle on the floor. And that, I cannot allow."

There, in the marquee at Kerem Shalom, I still do not grasp the full magnitude of the disaster that has befallen us. Neither my personal horrific losses, nor the scale of Hamas' massacre of civilians. Speaking with the casualty officer, I never get the sense that she is hiding something from me.

Eventually, the officer hands me a cell phone, and I call my children Yuval and Shaked, talking to them for the first time after more than fifty days of total isolation. The excitement on both ends of the line is overwhelming. We feel like we are floating, like we are being plugged back into the world. They are impatient to see us. I do not ask about Avshal, still believing he is a hostage in Gaza. Nor about Lilach and Tari. But they know. And they say nothing.

After the initial intake process in the marquee, we are called to board a coach to the Sheba Medical Center outside Tel Aviv for medical examinations. Yula and Naveh climb aboard with colorful backpacks, Yula clutching a new teddy bear, which will keep her company for the coming weeks. The four of us sit together on the back row of the coach, the children placing their bulging bags of gifts at their feet: colorful chalk markers, drawing pads, unicorn dolls, and bubble toys. Sharon and Noam sit together a few rows away from us. I think of the soap bubbles in Gaza, how everything is different now. Now we are home, free. I surrender to this feeling of inebriation.

The coach sets out at midnight, packed with newly released hostages and their chaperones, creating a cheerful racket. Suddenly, we notice that at every intersection, despite the very late hour, there are hundreds of people standing and waving Israeli flags at us. This is our first glimpse of the waves of joy that are sweeping through Israel amid the ongoing release of hostages.

During the drive, I wonder whether the coach will pass the intersection at the entrance to Kibbutz Be'eri. I have always cherished that spot. In my childhood, it signaled a return from family trips and vacations; in adulthood, it meant I was back from my travels around the world, back to Avshal, to my children and friends, to the home where I had lived all my life. But this time, I am afraid we will pass this spot, fearful of having to cross the site where I saw enough to understand the carnage that was unfolding on October 7.

I feel immense relief when the bus driver, knowingly or not, chooses a different route to the hospital in central Israel.

The driver turns on the radio, and I catch fragments of heated debates about the hostage release deal. Passionate voices for and against the deal blast out of the speakers, alongside reports of fatalities and casualties. I firmly ask that the radio be turned off. We are not yet ready to deal with what is happening around us. The officer immediately approaches the driver, and quiet returns.

Before reaching the Sheba Medical Center, we stop to stretch our legs at a gas station, where I am surprised to see a neighbor from Kibbutz Be'eri: Yair Rotem, one of my and Avshal's close friends. Yair is the uncle of thirteen-year-old Hila Rotem, who was released today without her mother, his sister, after the terrorists cruelly separated them in Gaza. He received special permission to meet Hila at Kerem Shalom and is driving her up in a separate vehicle.

Despite the darkness, Yair recognizes me, approaches me in a fluster, and holds me tight in a long embrace. "You have no idea what your son did for you," he says. "He organized a massive march for the hostages' release and got the whole country on its feet." In this moment, I cannot grasp the scale of what our Yuval, aged thirty-seven, created and led in the effort to secure our release.

Before October 7, Yuval was a shy, reserved man. Only weeks after our return do friends describe to me in greater detail how he suddenly opened up, how he riled up huge crowds with passion and confidence, how he led tens of thousands of people from Tel Aviv to Jerusalem in the first march for the hostages' freedom.

When the bus arrives at the hospital around 2:00 a.m., there are hundreds of people standing around the large traffic circle at the entrance to the hospital complex. Some are doctors and nurses; others are ordinary people who came to support us. Once again, it is staggering to see the solidarity and excitement our release has ignited among Israelis. Men and women are cheering or weeping. Some are doing both.

We are escorted into the hospital under tight security, this time to shield us from reporters, cameras, and prying eyes. Only authorized photographers are allowed to cover what is happening, and we retain the right to decide what will or will not be published. The hospital has put strict security procedures in place within the inpatient department to ensure our privacy. Entry is permitted only to medical staff, military escorts, and close family members.

As we exit the elevator, we are led to our assigned room, and there, finally, we see Yuval and Shaked, nine months pregnant. My three children and I cling to each other in a powerful, four-way embrace of immense relief and release from pent-up tension, caught in a rapture of laughter and tears.

Beside us, Grandpa Gilad, Tal's father, hoists Naveh and Yula into the air again and again in his longing, joyful arms, as Nitza, their other grandma, hugs them.

In all the commotion, I am not surprised that Avshal is not there. I knew that we surrendered and left the safe room together. Throughout captivity, I believed Hamas was holding him hostage somewhere else in the Gaza Strip. Since I assumed that women and children would be released first, I reasoned he and Tal would be included only in later stages of the deal.

Sharon and Noam were given a separate room of their own. In our spacious room there are four beds, each covered with crisp white sheets, premium blankets, and plump pillows. Beside them are huge red duffel bags with basic clothing, pajamas, underwear, and toiletries. Soft slippers await us at the foot of each bed.

On our pillows, Adi and I find cardboard boxes wrapped in cellophane, containing new cellphones, reconnecting us to the world. Only after turning on my new device do I realize that it does not contain my WhatsApp and SMS history. I have no way of seeing my cries for help to the world on the morning of October 7, or my messages with my beloved Avshal.

On Yula's bed are unicorn dolls, some from their family home in Ma'ale Tzviya; others are gifts from strangers moved by our return. Among the unicorns sits a hand-knitted teddy bear to which Yula was especially attached. But now she prefers to cling to the teddy bear she received at Kerem Shalom.

On Naveh's bed lie three soccer jerseys: One of Argentina's national team, with Messi's number ten; one of Hapoel Be'er Sheva, the team he supports because of Grandpa Avshal; and one of Bayern Munich, with his name on the back, a kind gesture from the German club to the child hostage.

Within a minute, Naveh has already swapped into his Messi jersey and starts playing in the ward with a worn red-and-white ball. I am later told that the ball was found outside our destroyed home in Be'eri, along with one of the two soccer shoes Naveh had brought to the kibbutz. The other did not survive. Search teams also found Avshal's favorite cooking pot, scorched by the heat, and a family heirloom menorah. Shaked's husband, Daniel, who is religiously observant, was deeply moved to find it among the ruins.

Meanwhile, the second wave of well-wishers arrives: my brothers, David and Aviv. David, the eldest, true to form as the son of a (famously sticklerish) German Jew and a mother we nicknamed "Sparta," is inexpressive. He gives me a firm hug and explains that when we arrived, they were asked to hide behind a partition so as not to overwhelm us. But Aviv cannot hide his emotions. He gives me a long hug and says, "The whole time you were in Gaza, I pictured you like our mother, getting by and surviving through pure grit."

In our reunion, he captures exactly what I felt there in Gaza.

Then I notice that Lilach, our youngest sister, is not in the room.

I understand: She is gone.

I understand it without words, because in the first minutes after we were kidnapped, as the terrorists marched us at gunpoint with their AK-47s, I saw Lilach and Tari's house blown apart, its roof crushed, smoke billowing out. I knew they could not escape because of Tari's medical condition; also, our WhatsApp chat had gone cold about an hour before we surrendered.

And yet, throughout captivity, I kept a small ember of hope that maybe, just maybe, the safe room had saved them. I dare not ask David and Aviv about her fate, and they dare not raise it. Both they and I understand that the news is still impossible to share. It is all still so turbulent, so overwhelming, so sensitive. The dissonance between the world of yesterday and now is too painful to reconcile.

Yuval tells me that he and Shaked had been running between optometrists to track down my prescription and bought me new glasses. When they watch me getting released on television and realized I had returned with my own glasses, they breathed a sigh of relief.

Yuval, who has thought of every detail to cheer me up after what I went through, has also brought an automatic coffee machine to the hospital, exactly like the one we had at home. At this point, I still I do not know that our own machine was either vaporized in the explosion or looted into Gaza. Yuval, such a sensitive boy, also remembered to bring my favorite coffee beans and mug. At last, I can pamper myself with quality coffee, just like at home in Be'eri.

A stream of doctors from different specialties come to see us. I notice that all the medical staff are wearing dog tags like those worn by IDF soldiers, except that these ones are engraved with the words "Our heart is captive in Gaza." These dog tags are another expression of the profound sense of identity many Israelis feel with the suffering of the hostages and the urgent need to bring them home.

Gradually, more family members join us: Shaked's husband, Daniel, and Anna-Lee, Yuval's girlfriend, who moved in with him in Be'eri only three months before that fateful day. Fortunately, on October 6, they had gone to meet friends in the desert, so were away from the kibbutz during the massacre.

Later, Tal's siblings, Mor and Lee, also arrive. Then Ronen, Avshal's brother, who lives in Australia, followed by Ruth, Avshal's mother, who lived right next to us in Be'eri in recent years but managed to survive that cursed day. Chen, Sharon's husband, and their son Omer are with her and Noam in a separate room, and later, they join us as well.

The experience is emotionally overwhelming. We are all talking over each other, and from snippets of information, I try to piece together an initial picture of what happened while we were gone. The journey we have made in the last eighteen hours—from the doctor's apartment in the heart of Gaza, entirely at the mercy of armed terrorists, to Israel, surrounded by loved ones who worked day and night to secure our release—is impossible to fathom.

We are exhausted, and at around 4:00 a.m., we prepare for a short sleep. I decide to give up my private room and stay to sleep with Adi and the grandchildren, a matter of habit after we were pressed together for fifty nights.

The next morning, we undergo a series of medical tests to assess the damage caused by captivity. We need to give blood samples. This is three-and-a-half-year-old Yula's first blood test, and she is terrified. Adi and I accompany her to the testing room, with a full team of smiling nurses and a pediatrician. There is even a medical clown to distract her, and eventually she relents.

A few days after we are discharged, Yula asks Adi, "Mommy, after every vacation, when we come back, will they do blood tests on us?" I shudder at the question and think to myself, *What has this sweet, angelic child had to endure?* What scars will remain from the pogrom she witnessed in Be'eri? From captivity? Adi explains to her that we are in a safe place now, and there will be no need for tests when we return from future vacations.

On our first morning in the hospital, I savor the freedom to decide at every moment what to do and where to be, having been subjected to such total deprivation of liberty for so long. I switch on the coffee maker and sip a mug of a quality brew, feeling the pleasure I had yearned for washing over me.

Afterward, we all gather for breakfast, a smorgasbord of vegetables, cheeses, omelets, and bread. As we eat, I notice Yula taking a small tub of cottage cheese and dividing it into two similar-sized mounds, a habit she developed in captivity to ensure each child received an equal helping. Adi explains there is no need for that anymore. She can take as much as she wants.

CHAPTER XI
CONFRONTING LOSS

THEN COMES THE MOST TERRIBLE moment of all. Shaked and Yuval ask me to join them in my private room. Through choked voices and tears, they tell me that my beloved Avshal, their father, is not being held hostage by Hamas after all.

He was murdered in Be'eri on that black Saturday.

The news strikes me like the blade of a cold, sharp ax. The only thing I manage to say is, "I know if he had a choice, to save us or himself, he would have chosen to save us." This much I have always known in the depths of my heart, even before that dark day. From forty years of splendid partnership. From our shared understanding of what truly matters: children, family, life. And that is exactly how he acted on October 7. First, in his decision to stay outside the safe room with a kitchen knife, and then, when he joined us inside and bolted the door shut with all his might even as the terrorists' bullets pierced through.

Avshal and Tal risked their lives to save ours. And I understand that the same supreme purpose led them both to surrender as soon as the terrorists managed to wrench open the steel plates of the safe-room window. They understood that if we did not surrender at once, the terrorists would hurl a grenade inside and kill us all.

These flashbacks meld into the horrific news I have just received. It is still incomprehensible. Yuval and Shaked go on to tell me that in the first days of the war, the IDF believed that Avshal had also been taken to Gaza, and we were all classified as hostages. But eleven days after the attack, his body was identified. He was murdered in the place he loved so much, the place *we* loved so much, the place where we built our lives together.

They tell me the funeral was held at the cemetery in his teenage hometown of Omer, near Be'er Sheva. Thousands of people—extended family, friends, and acquaintances—came from all over Israel to accompany him on his final journey.

I understand what they are telling me, but the words do not sink in. The tears are trapped inside me. I cannot face the loss. Only one thing is clear to me, even in these awful moments: From now on, I must be strong for them, for our children, for our grandchildren. I must be the one to hold everything together.

Alone.

We sit in the room, engulfed in pain and love, trying to steady each other, clinging to the fact that we are finally together after fifty days of terror and uncertainty. They already buried their father more than a month ago, sat shiva as a broken family, surrounded by relatives and friends. And here I am, back from another world, where I held myself together with a single-minded focus on surviving, on protecting the other half of my family.

And now the full force of the catastrophe drops onto me.

After a few minutes I say, "Lilach didn't come yesterday with David and Aviv. I gather she didn't survive." And Shaked and

Yuval, tears streaming down their faces, are forced to confirm the bitter truth. Tari and his caregiver, Paul, were also murdered that day. Paul's wife, Jubal, was nine months pregnant at the time. She gave birth to their firstborn son soon after the attack and named him Paul, after the father who did not live to see him.

I am swept up in a whirlwind of emotions. On the one hand, I am confronted with the unbearable news of the deaths of Avshal, Lilach, Tari, and Paul, and of the terrorist atrocities in Be'eri. On the other, I am happy that everyone who was with me in captivity came back alive, that I completed the mission I set for myself.

As I write these lines, over a year and a half after the October 7 terror attack, I learn from our close friend Yarona that in his final moments, Avshal managed to save others from the inferno. Reading her text message, my stomach turns. Yarona writes that she heard this from Eti, the mother of Ohad—a young man who had gone to the Nova festival to celebrate with his friends, Amir and Gal.

Eti herself gives me the full rundown of the dramatic events. She worked with Avshal for years and, like many, became a close friend.

At their family dinner on Friday, October 6, when Ohad told her that he was planning to go to a party not far from Be'eri, she felt a surge of anxiety. The proximity to the Gaza border meant a risk of rocket fire. At that time, our fears were confined to the skies; a full-scale ground invasion was beyond our darkest nightmares and was simply never a scenario anyone considered possible. She called Avshal immediately, and he told her, "Don't be hysterical, let the kid go. Relax. It's fine." When she told him she still felt uneasy, he added, "Listen, the army and the police approved the event. Besides, give him my number. We have a big safe room, and if anything happens, he can come to us with his friends. If you need, you can even wake me up in the middle of the night."

Ohad and his friends drove south, and Eti called him anxiously at 2:00 a.m. and asked him to update her when they arrive safely at the festival grounds. At 3:30 a.m., he called her and said, "Mom, the army's here, we've got police and ambulances, and there's even a tank. Everything's fine."

At 6:29 a.m., when the sirens blared across Israel, she called Ohad, and he told her the rocket fire from Gaza was insane and they were planning to head out to Tel Aviv, hoping this would put them out of rocket range.

Still on edge, she called Avshal, who WhatsApped her our home location. At 7:10 a.m., he texted her, "Stay calm. The Iron Dome is working well, and in any case I'm leaving the safe room open for them."

Eti forwarded the location to Ohad, and he wrote back that something seriously dramatic was happening in the area and they realized they would never make it to Tel Aviv. So they decided to drive to Be'eri instead.

At 8:29 a.m., Avshal sent Eti a message: "Tell him not to come. The kibbutz is swarming with hundreds of terrorists." She called him back, and he answered, agitated: "Tell them to stay away! He should go home!" Seconds later, Avshal called Ohad himself and warned him to stay clear of Be'eri.

Disappointed, Ohad called his mother and said Avshal had turned them away. "Trust Avshal and do as he says," she told him. So Ohad and his friends abandoned the car at the side of the road and ran through the fields in a blind sprint to the east, until they reached Patish, an agricultural village eleven miles from Be'eri, exhausted and shaken but alive and safe.

When Eti tells me all this, I think about how naive we were, how blind we were, and also how typical it was of Avshal to help his friends and their children however he could. He was a man who gave with all his heart.

***

I leave my room into the corridor and see Avida Bachar, a friend from Be'eri, rolling toward me energetically in a wheelchair. I notice that his left leg has been amputated. He reaches me and I bend down to give him a long, tight hug. We go over to the coffee station, and there he describes what happened to his family on that terrible day, October 7.

At 6:30 a.m., after the sirens sounded, they went into their safe room—Avida; his wife, Dana, a beloved kindergarten teacher at my grandson Naveh's previous daycare; and their two children, Carmel, fifteen, and Hadar, thirteen.

When the terrorists broke into their home, Avida and Carmel gripped the handle of the safe room door, even as bullets pierced it and wounded both of them. The terrorists lit a fire outside the door, and they began to choke on the smoke that was seeping into the safe room. Even so, they held the door shut. The terrorists left the house, blew up the safe room window from the outside, shot Dana, and threw three grenades inside. Toward noon, after hours of torment, Dana succumbed to her wounds. Carmel held on until 5:00 p.m. before she bled to death. Avida was left with Hadar. Only at 7:30 p.m. did IDF soldiers come to rescue them.

As Avida reconstructs the horrors that he and his family suffered, I think: *If Avshal and Tal had not decided to surrender the moment our safe-room window was breached, we would have met the same fate.*

Avida goes on to tell me that during his rehabilitation in the hospital, he lay in a bed next to a religious man covered in burns all over his body. Every time the nurses came to change his bandages, he would thank God out loud. "I asked him, why are you thanking God? You're suffering in hell," Avida said. The man answered, "I bless what remains. What I have, and what I had."

Avida was deeply touched by that approach and embraced it. "I'm grateful for every moment I had with Dana," he tells me, "and for the fifteen wonderful years I was blessed to live with Carmel. I bless everyone who is still alive and chooses to look forward."

I am in awe of his vitality, his bounty of positive energy, but I am still in a different place. In these hours, I am still in shock, still in the first stages of grappling with the disaster that befell us. That befell me.

Later that day, Alon Haberfeld, the CEO of Fair Planet, comes to visit with his wife, Hagit. We share a long embrace. I find that complex emotions can also be conveyed through touch, through hugs, through eye contact.

Sometimes words are unnecessary.

The first thing Alon tells me about is the open day in Rwanda. "I knew you wouldn't forgive us if we canceled it," he says. The event did not take place exactly as I had imagined in captivity, because flights from Israel to Rwanda were canceled in the first days of the war (a scenario that did not cross my mind in Gaza), but the organization's local team and the Israeli embassy staff in Kigali hosted a successful event with local farmers and guests from around the world. Alon also tells me how many of our colleagues in seed companies around the world mobilized to campaign for our release.

After my visitors leave the ward, we receive representatives from the Interior Ministry to issue us new ID cards and passports in place of the ones that were burned in the house. They take my photo right after I receive an injection in my left eye, which had been operated on several times before I was kidnapped and was not treated properly in captivity. The photo is, of course, awful, but the desire to return immediately to the status of a free citizen with an identity is overwhelming. I can take another, more presentable photo later.

My new ID card arrives within two hours, and my heart skips a beat. There, in black and white, next to "relationship status," it reads: "Widow." It has only been a few hours since my children told me Avshal was murdered, and already I have a new official status. It hurts. It is cruel. It is unfathomable.

At some point in the afternoon, Yuval asks whether I would be willing to meet with the families of other hostages from Be'eri who are still held in Gaza. I oblige. We go down to the administrative floor, where the hospital has booked us a conference room that's far larger than we need. In the center is a huge wooden oval table surrounded by about twenty office chairs, and the walls are lined with bookcases packed with medical volumes.

They enter gingerly: Ella, the daughter of Ohad Ben Ami, who lived in the neighborhood next to mine on the kibbutz, and Merav and Yuval Svirsky, the children of Orit, my beloved adjoining neighbor. The terrorists murdered Orit minutes before they entered our house. Her son Itay, who was visiting her that morning, witnessed her murder and was abducted to Gaza. None of us know at this point what will become of him. In the end, he survives ninety-nine days in captivity before his captors shoot him when an IDF force approaches their hiding place. The thought of his agonizing, utterly avoidable death leaves his family no respite. Nor does it leave me a moment's peace.

Merav, Yuval, and Ella ask me to tell them everything I know. Orit's children want more and more details about the horror that unfolded in her home. I tell them what I heard from next door that morning: the gunfire, the explosions, the shattering glass.

As for the conditions in captivity, I tell them I can describe only what we experienced and emphasize that this does not necessarily represent how other hostages may be held. They are hungry for every word, and I keep talking and talking. We part, still gripped with that heavy, sinking feeling.

After the meeting, Adi and I set up our new replacement cellphones. We consult with security officers about whether to keep our old numbers or switch to new ones, and we decide the advantages of keeping our original numbers outweigh the risks that hostile actors might try to abuse them to harm us. In hindsight, this decision proves to be a mistake, at least for Adi. Months after our release, while Tal is still being held in tunnels dozens of feet underground, she receives disturbing calls threatening his life. The investigation shows the anonymous callers were phoning from Gaza, probably on Hamas' orders.

Gila, my brother Aviv's wife, comes to visit in the hospital and brings me some good fresh clothes so I can change out of the tracksuits donated by such generous strangers. Over time, these donated clothes become a source of humor. We invent a fashion line called "La Palitte," which sounds like a high-end French label inspired by Galeries Lafayette, but is really Hebrew for "refugee."

Because that is what we are now.

Between all the tests and administrative tasks, the hospital staff invite the children who survived captivity to a performance by a singer who came to cheer them up. Naveh goes to watch with Grandpa Gilad and Grandma Nitza, while Yula stays glued to Adi. She refuses to let go of her for even a moment.

During the day, our blood test results arrive. It turns out we have all lost weight and are suffering from severe malnutrition. Our blood tests point to significant mineral and vitamin deficiencies, so we are all prescribed food supplements and medications for at least a month.

In the late afternoon, the hospital staff update us that the next day we can move to an adjacent hotel or find another living arrangement. Yuval tells us that he and Anna-Lee are currently living in a spacious house in Herzliya, owned by a British Jewish family who generously made it available to support the families of hostages. Now we can all stay there together and have privacy, shielded from the media and onlookers. We decide to move there.

After packing our belongings and the pile of gifts we received, we fill the trunks of two cars and finally set out as free people. We breathe in the air of freedom, so new to us, riding in our own cars—not Hamas or Red Cross vehicles—toward an uncertain future and a long, painful journey of healing and recovery.

On the way, we pass familiar intersections, and I notice Israeli flags flying at all of them and large signs with photos of us and the other hostages with the text: “BRING THEM HOME NOW!”

As we drive along the Ayalon Highway, Yula’s face suddenly appears on a giant digital billboard on the façade of a tower. The sweet little girl, whose parents always protected her privacy and avoided posting her photos on social media, is now a poster girl of this essential cause. No one asked Adi or Tal because there was no one to ask. They were in captivity too. But there is no doubt that under the circumstances they would have agreed.

The expressions of support for our release move us deeply. At the entrance to Herzliya, we see an enormous number of yellow ribbons tied to tree trunks, utility poles, and house gates. Yuval explains that after the mass kidnappings of October 7, the yellow ribbon became the symbol of the hostages in Israel, and it is common to see people wearing yellow lapel pins and sticking the yellow ribbon emblem on their cars.

And through all of it, I keep thinking about Tal, still languishing in captivity, praying he will come back as soon as possible, and about Avshal and Lilach and Tari. The pain of their loss begins to seep in slowly, and I know it will be many months before I can begin to absorb this gaping, terrible absence.

CHAPTER XII
AVSHAL

ADI, NAVEH, YULAH, AND I enter a broad pedestrian promenade paved with mosaics and bordered by neat landscaping. At the far end, the sea comes into view, illuminated by the sun's rays as evening draws near. On both sides of the promenade stand four-story buildings divided into garden apartments and spacious penthouses.

We walk into the garden apartment where Yuval and Anna-Lee are already living. They give us a tour that begins in the beautiful living room, continues through six bedrooms, goes down to the basement level with its private cinema and reclining armchairs, and then returns to a manicured yard furnished with a glass table, wicker chairs, and a large hot tub.

I cannot help but think of the gaping difference between our conditions in captivity and the intoxicating freedom and comfort we have just landed into.

Meanwhile, the appetizing aromas of home cooking waft our way. Relatives have brought us delicacies of every kind, and a pot of fragrant vegetable soup simmers on the stove. We sit around a marble dining table with a fresh flower arrangement at the center. Only then do I notice that on a shelf in the wall niche opposite us are framed photographs of Avshal, and beneath them, memorial candles. I stop breathing. I was not prepared for such a direct encounter with my loss.

I look straight ahead at the photographs. In one of them, the two of us are standing embraced on the romantic Pont Neuf over the Seine in Paris in October 2022, exactly one year before the horrific massacre. We lean into each other, Avshal's arm around my shoulders, mine around his waist, both of us looking into the camera Yuval is holding: loving, relaxed, secure.

That photograph was taken on a trip we invited Yuval and Anna-Lee to join. We were so happy together, the two of us with the happy young couple. Memories start flooding back from that vacation, and only now do I begin to understand it was our last.

What you cannot see in the picture is the brown shopping bag on the stone paving of the bridge. That magical morning, as we walked along Rue Mouffetard near the Sorbonne, I spotted a set of coffee cups in the window of a houseware store. Even though it was only the start of a grueling day of crossing Paris on foot, I bought twelve porcelain cups, and Avshal carried the heavy bag for the rest of the day.

I feel a pinch in my chest when I reflect that Avshal always, *always* indulged every whim of mine, just to make me happy. On another trip we took together to Italy's Amalfi Coast, we discovered local artisans who build and paint tables made from black lava. I fell in love with a round, shockingly heavy table painted with yellow lemons against an ultramarine background. Without hesitation, Avshal carried it around on foot, then got it in the car and eventually on the plane, and we brought it home to Be'eri. I placed it beside a yellow armchair by the large window that looked out onto our beautiful garden. Today, it is all ashes. Gone. Destroyed. Nothing remains.

In the other photographs on the shelf, Avshal is pictured playing soccer with Naveh on the grass in Be'eri, splashing in the pool with Yula, laughing with Shaked's children, Nahar-Shalom and Sinai-Moshe. He loved his grandchildren so much, and they adored him. I miss him so much.

After the meal, more family members and close friends arrive. Everyone is eager to hear what each and every one of us went through.

We go out into the yard and sit around the big table. And then I start talking, and talking, and talking. The words pour out without pause for breath, and as I reconstruct our story for the first time, I realize I will have to repeat it again and again and again. Because of the immense emotional toll, each time I will have to shorten it, leave out some more details, until eventually even my memory fades and the stories lose their luster.

When our friends and relatives disperse, we go to bed. The sheets are clean and soft, and we burrow under warm blankets. The foldout bed in the basement, where I choose to sleep so I can stay close to Adi and the grandchildren, is surprisingly comfortable.

But the memories keep flooding back and give me no respite. The massacre in Be'eri, our unpleasant experiences in captivity, my terrible grief over the murders of Avshal, Lilach, Tari, and so many others from our small community—all these swirl together in my mind.

At the hospital, I was offered sleeping pills to help me fall asleep. I take one, and a soothing sense of disconnection seizes my body and my mind. I float on the waves of the comforting pill and sink into a deep slumber.

The following day, family and friends keep coming all day long. It feels like a shiva, people constantly entering and leaving, bringing food and drinks of every kind. But unlike a real shiva, no one speaks about the dead. About Avshal. And I feel like I am in a bizarre movie scene, where everything is unfolding around me, but the plot goes nowhere. We avoid the pain, drawing endless circles around the elephant in the room.

In the late afternoon, two couples of close friends arrive: Tomer Amir and his wife Ayelet Hirshman, and Aliza Goren and her husband Danny Rothschild. After much hugging and vigorous shoulder patting, we sit in the yard. As coffee and snacks are served, I remember a small detail from my former life.

I remember how much I loved picking up our children from the airport when they returned from trips abroad. During the drive back to Be'eri, which took about an hour and a half, they regaled me with the freshest, fullest version of their experiences. The intimacy of sharing the confined space of the car, usually late at night, was a precious time bubble that could never be replicated, when I got to hear, in minute detail, about my children's encounters with new cultures and people, about what they felt and tasted, their adventures and fears. I knew there was nothing like sharing a story for the first time, before the return to routine blurred their memories and repetition and time wore them down.

Suddenly, I clock the enormous importance of giving testimony while the feelings and the memories are still fresh. I ask Tomer whether he could record our conversation. I know that some of what I am about to say will be considered classified by Israeli security agencies, so I ask him to record our conversation on his iPhone and make sure it never leaves that device.

I describe everything I remember, in the greatest detail and with the most minimal restraint, skipping between times, emotions, and factual accounts. They sit opposite me, alert and intent, and every so often I ask: *Should I stop? Are you sure this isn't too much?* They ask me to continue. The recording lasts more than two and a half hours, and I know it will serve as the basis for a more orderly eyewitness account, when I am able to confront it—when I can finally put into writing everything that happened to us in those terrible days.

The knowledge that my testimony has been recorded and securely saved—it remains that way for more than a year—allows me to return my focus to the present and to this new battle for survival that I have been thrown into. Without Avshal, without Lilach, without the support I had all those years with both of them beside me. Support that is gone forever.

I still cannot grasp that I have no home. That I am homeless in the full sense of the word. I still cannot absorb that I have no clothes that are truly mine. None of the treasured objects I collected over the years. None of the jewelry passed down through generations of my family.

I wake in the morning, open my eyes to this foreign ceiling, this temporary cover, and feel an endless rage. All that remains of my previous life is the memories. And they burn, fizzle, slip away, rush back, washing over me in waves of sorrow and anger.

***

It is very hard for me to put into words the love and relationship I had with Avshal. We were so different, yet we complemented each other perfectly. We met while studying for our undergraduate degrees at the Rehovot campus of the Hebrew University.

I was a model student who attended every lecture and took meticulous notes. He was working three different jobs at the time, only popped in for some of the classes, and covered the material himself with a few study buddies, mainly in the run-up to exams.

Many of our friends raised an eyebrow when we became a couple, but we quickly formed a powerful bond as two independent people who gave each other space to grow and breathe. After a long trip around the world, we decided to marry and settle in Kibbutz Be'eri, where I had already planted roots. This was not a natural choice for Avshal, who preferred the lively rhythm of a big city, preferably Tel Aviv.

I always used to laugh about it and tease him, "Look how much you love me, so much that you agreed to live somewhere so different from what appealed to you!" But Avshal found a way to combine life in a cooperative kibbutz far from Israel's big cities with his professional and personal development. He moved onwards and upwards in business, held senior management positions, and in the end, Tel Aviv became his professional home anyway.

And now the pain strikes with full force. After all, *I'm* the one who drew him to live so close to Gaza. It's because of *me* we lived within walking distance of the border. And then the worst happened. He was murdered by terrorists who overran our kibbutz. I am overcome with guilt, intertwined with frustration and rage at how we were abandoned. I know he liked his own life. I know none of us ever imagined we might be attacked like this. But the thoughts refuse to leave me. And the sense of responsibility hurts so much.

Avshal had a rare gift. He read people like an open book. He had the finely tuned senses of a seismograph. With unusual intuition and a singular talent, he formed deep friendships and maintained them for years. Even in our marriage, he detected and read my thoughts before I could even put them into words.

Avshal was a man of the night, and I was a woman of the morning. When we drove back late at night after meetings or evenings out in the city, he loved taking the scenic route to Be'eri. When we were still a young couple, I stayed awake on those nighttime drives and tried to talk with him to keep him alert. But in time, I allowed myself to doze while he drove and listen to the music he loved. Later, I would recline the seat back to sleep more comfortably, until eventually I even started using those eye masks they hand out on planes. I used to wake only when the car stopped outside our home on the kibbutz. I remember how we laughed about it. We called it "the evolution of married life."

Not long after I am released from captivity, I am invited to meet some family friends. After some hesitation, I decide to emerge from my hermit-like confinement and go. On the way back, driving alone through the emptiness of the night, sitting in the driver's seat with "my" seat to the right of me, empty, I am flooded with grief for everything that was and will not return—for his life, for our life together.

In these days, I also think of Lilach, and of the joy we shared in life together in Be'eri. We had been close for sixty years, from the day she was born until October 7. I loved being her older sister; eight years her senior, I watched her grow from a sweet, smiling baby into a freckled, energetic child. Even at that tender age, I recognized her sensitivity, her caring, her compassion for others. As she grew older and the age gap seemed to shrink, people sometimes confused us, especially when we chose the same haircut. They used to call me Lilach and her Shoshan, and we both roared at the mix-ups.

In temperament, we were different. I chose the natural sciences, following my father, a doctor of entomology who worked in biological pest control and sanitation. I specialized in plant sciences and worked in seed development and international aid. Lilach pursued a career in therapy, helping people and alleviating human distress. From an early age, she was exceptionally sensitive to the suffering of others, and naturally she chose to study social work, specializing in art therapy and psychotherapy. For many years, she worked at the local council's resilience center, was active with at-risk youth, and even welcomed into her heart and home young women she mentored through these programs. She also volunteered with INBAL[7] and MASLAN[8], two organizations that assist survivors of sexual assault and violence. I always admired her ability to alleviate people's pain and offer them solace and grace, while I worked with plants and the hands-on work of international aid.

At the heart of her work was trauma therapy. She was always looking for creative ways to help each person find strength and calm within themselves, using games and movement exercises, practicing the methods she believed in with the children in her care. As part of her work at the resilience center, she wrote a book titled *The Trigger Song*, later republished as *About Those Startling Sounds*[9]. The book grew out of her many years

---

7 Inbal Center, Treatment and Assistance for Victims of Sexual Abuse. Yachdav Association. Retrieved from https://www.yachdav.org.il/לבנע

8 Maslan, Negev Sexual Assault and Domestic Violence Support Center. Available at https://www.maslan.org.il

9 Kipnis, L. *About Those Startling Sounds*. Privately published; made possible by donor contributions. Audio version available at https://www.youtube.com/watch?v=y_FhlmVqf4A

of therapy sessions with children from the Gaza border region. After years of rocket and mortar fire, Lilach wanted to validate these frightened children's fears instead of telling them "It's nothing." In the book's recurring refrain, she wrote: "Don't be afraid, you are protected now. Everything is all right here. Now you can relax, gradually let go, take a deep breath, and drink a little, choose what makes you feel good."

Appropriately for a therapist, she never told us what happened inside the therapy room. Only after her death did we hear from patients how important she was to them. Because of her personal touch, every patient was sure Lilach was "theirs" alone, that she could not possibly have given herself like that to other patients too. But she gave to everyone and changed the lives of so many.

Lilach's book promises that her words of wisdom will never fall silent. It continues to inspire parents, teachers, and educators, offering support to children all over the country. Between its pages, the fingerprints of her warm, good, wise hands are impossible to miss.

Lilach's sensitivity and empathy also shaped her political views. While studying at the Hebrew University in Jerusalem, she joined Women in Black, an international movement known for its silent anti-war protests. Every week, she stood in Paris Square in Jerusalem across from Beit Aghion, the prime minister's residence, to demonstrate against human rights violations by Israelis in the West Bank, and to mourn all victims of the conflict. Later, she also joined Women Wage Peace.

I recall how much Lilach loved her family—her husband Tari and children Yotam and Nadav—and how our bond deepened as we cared for our parents together as they aged. Both of our parents lived to ninety-six and died with a sense of fulfillment, seeing

Kibbutz Be'eri thrive and their family expand into a sprawling clan, replete with grandchildren and great-grandchildren.

After they passed away, we used to visit their graves nearly every week, water the plants around the headstones, and clean the letters engraved in marble that captured the essence of their lives. It was there that we would have our heart-to-heart talks. This weekly visit to the cemetery became our quality time together, and I believed and hoped we would continue like this for many years to come, growing older side by side.

Lilach celebrated her sixtieth birthday in August 2023, only two months before she was murdered. As a birthday gift to herself, she decided to learn Arabic directly from native speakers in the Bedouin city of Rahat. There, with the help of local women, she also refined her cooking and baking skills, another activity she loved and excelled in.

At her birthday party, Tari raised a charming toast. It was another expression of their deeply impressive partnership. They shared a harmony and common interests. Like Lilach, Tari also enjoyed spending time in the kitchen. He was a stickler for good coffee, which he ground and poured from a large vintage machine, and he even brewed his own beer at home.

Tari was born on Kibbutz Ma'agan Michael, a boy of the sea who later served in the Israeli navy and then sailed the high seas as a skipper. His masterful touch, technical mind, and sweeping knowledge made him a sought-after yacht captain. Later he studied metalwork at the Bezalel Academy of Arts, where he met Lilach, who was also studying in Jerusalem at the time.

After debating between the two kibbutzim, they decided to settle in Be'eri, far from the waves of Ma'agan Michael, and Tari compensated for the loss by going out on Saturdays to paddle on a kayak at Nitzanim Beach.

Their home was open and welcoming. Whenever we dropped by, we were greeted by homemade cookies or exquisite cakes fresh from the oven, and we often joined them for a Shabbat meal. For dessert, we devoured conversations about what was going on around the kibbutz, seasoned with local gossip.

They were hosts by nature: Everything from the traditional winter reunion of Tari's friends from the navy to their stuffed grape leaf workshops led by Majida, an Arab woman from East Jerusalem who became a close friend of Lilach's and often came to Be'eri with her wonderful daughters.

When Tari was fifty-seven, he was diagnosed with a chronic illness that weakened the muscles in his limbs. He was hospitalized for treatments, then sent for long-term rehabilitation that included an art class, where he discovered his new passion. The strong man once known for a handshake that could crush a grown man's hand began holding a paintbrush in fingers that were not always steady, but his great talent triumphed over his disability. Sea creatures and boats, scenes of tranquility and the scorching sun in the western Negev—he drew inspiration from every stop on his life and imprinted them on canvas.

He was a man of peace, an atheist whose religion was respect and giving to others, his heart open to every fellow human. He donated the treatment bed he received to a hospital in Gaza. Throughout his years of illness, he continued helping Israelis in the south of the country manage their finances efficiently by volunteering with the Paamonim, a nonprofit that supports families experiencing financial difficulties. He also mentored young people in sailing.

Paul Vincent Castelvi, his dedicated caregiver from the Philippines, was more than just a companion; he was his driver, his "hands and legs" when needed, and the one who pushed him to keep exercising even when it was difficult. Lilach stayed by their side, offering constant support and love. Paul was murdered by Hamas on October 7, one of seven foreign nationals killed in Kibbutz Be'eri alone. He was part of a larger, harrowing toll: Throughout the day, over seventy foreign nationals from more than thirty countries were massacred, exposing the indiscriminate nature of an attack that targeted anyone who stood in the terrorists' path.

Six days before October 7, Lilach and Tari returned from a river cruise in the south of France, where they were joined by Tari's sisters, Gaya and Tzafra, and their partners. Tari was at his best there, happy and active, unaware of what was lurking around the corner on the following Saturday. After his death, his paintings were collected in a wonderful exhibition and accompanying catalog titled *Chasing the Wind.* This collection titled "Striving for Spirit" was presented at the Daniel Center in Tel Aviv.

***

The day after our release from captivity, Aviv tells me that President Isaac Herzog is set to host a memorial for Lilach the following day. That morning, I rummage through the pile of donated clothes at the hospital and pick out blue jeans, a red T-shirt, and a black sweater. Not exactly presidential attire, but it is the best I had.

After we pass security at the entrance, I notice two bronze sculptures by Chana Orloff in the gardens of the President's Residence. Both depict strong, life-sized female figures: one sowing, the other binding sheaves of grain.

I am suddenly flooded with overwhelming emotion. I am in the middle of Jerusalem, in an institution that represents the heart of the State of Israel, and here are sculptures not only made by my great-aunt, who inspired me in captivity, but representing the power of women and the rock of human existence. Sowing, the primordial act that drives food production in the world, and harvesting, the final stage in the field before feeding.

Acts of creation, of hope.

We enter Beit HaNassi, the president's residence, and are received warmly by President Herzog and his wife, Michal. Miri Mesika—a singer of captivating talent and generosity—has come to honor my little sister's memory, dedicating Nurit Hirsh's 'The Lilac Flower' to her. Hot, heavy tears fill my eyes. This is the first time I allow myself to let go. And I cry.

After Miri Mesika's performance, Yotam, Lilach's eldest son, says, "Mom was not only a therapist: she demanded the long-term resolution of people's problems and took action to achieve that. Her book offers a personal, targeted solution for children who have experienced trauma, but the real answer is that the next generations should not have to experience that trauma."

Naomi Kamin from the Eshkol Resilience Center speaks about her love for Lilach and about the anguish she and her team have carried since the devastating events of October 7. She says the therapists had worked with children to reinforce their trust in the many layers that were meant to protect them: Trust in their parents to keep them safe; trust in the Red Alert siren system to blare as soon as a rocket is fired from Gaza; trust in safe rooms to provide protection through reinforced concrete walls and steel plates; trust in the emergency security squads in each community to hold off threats until the IDF arrives; trust in the Iron Dome to intercept rockets before they explode with destructive force; trust in the multibillion-dollar "smart fence" built on the Israel–Gaza border; and trust in the IDF to arrive quickly when needed. On October 7, that endless chain of supposed safety mechanisms entirely collapsed in real time.

And now, Naomi continues, the staff at the Resilience Center are wondering whether these reassuring messages contributed to normalizing a reality in which our enemies could fire rockets at our civilians while the state failed to respond with the necessary severity. Perhaps their therapeutic work acclimatized Israelis to extreme danger and made them accept it as normal.

As she speaks, I think to myself: Our acceptance of this abnormal reality was part of why the government and the IDF could effectively fall asleep at their posts, which is what led to the horrific results of October 7. I mull over the words "a sense of security," which we used so casually, and the penny drops—*that* is what they sold us all along. Not real security. A *sense* of security.

At the end of the event, Yuval, Aviv, and I move to a smaller room for a more intimate meeting with the president. I ask the video crew to switch off their cameras, and only then do I open up about our horrific experiences during the terrorists' invasion of Be'eri, about our abandonment, about the pogrom we suffered.

I also speak about our loss, as individuals and as a family, and about the catastrophe that befell my community in Be'eri. I ask that my words not be published because they are not the most important thing now. I know with absolute clarity that from now on, we need to act with all our strength to save my son-in-law Tal and all the other hostages left behind in Gaza.

Of the 251 people abducted on October 7, only 105 were released with us in the first deal, most of them women and children. Tal and another 145 hostages still need us to fight for them.

I ask the video crew to turn the cameras back on and say: "I'm already back, but there are still so many hostages in Gaza, and we must do everything we can so that everyone returns. I knew on my first day of captivity that my family and friends would jump into action within hours, doing everything they could to secure our release. I have complete faith in the State of Israel and the people of Israel that they are also doing everything in pursuit of that same goal."

It never occurs to me then that anyone might oppose the supremely important moral and ethical goal of redeeming hostages. I believe that everyone in Israel—the people, the government that abandoned us, the army that failed—will do anything to save the hostages.

Only now, as I write this, do I understand: The political polarization in Israel and the mutual distrust between its political factions have created an absurd situation. The nation finds itself confronted an ostensibly impossible dilemma: hostages or victory. In my view, this is not a dilemma; it is a complex reality flattened into a polarizing slogan. *The hostages can and must be saved.* This is a supreme value, a matter of mutual responsibility, a national obligation, and a prerequisite for Israel's security. There is no contradiction here, only complementarity. I am more convinced than ever that the hostages' return is not the end but the beginning of a process of healing—a renewal of the Israeli state's commitment to guard its borders and defend its citizens without compromise.

And I know one more thing: Many civilians in Gaza paid with their lives for the October 7 attack—residents caught in an urban battlefield, in areas bombed by the IDF while Hamas used them as human shields. I am often asked *Was anyone in Gaza truly uninvolved?* Are there people there who want and believe in peaceful coexistence? I have no authoritative answer. I can testify only on the basis of what I experienced. Witnessing life in Gaza forced me to confront a bleak reality in which the education system, under Hamas control, steers children from the most tender age toward hatred and jihadism.

That has to change.

CHAPTER XIII
STRUGGLE

IN THE EARLY EVENING, WE return to our temporary home in Herzliya, where family and friends await us. We begin to debate whether it is right to champion Tal's cause in the media, or whether focusing attention on him would only make Hamas raise the price for his release and make it harder to get him out. We wrestle with another question: Will the hostages' families' public campaign to bring them home help, or will it only weaken Israel's negotiating position?

We know that the hostages are being held by various groups—some by Hamas, some by Palestinian Islamic Jihad, and others by ordinary civilians. They are scattered across private houses and within the concrete tunnels that crisscross the Gaza Strip. We have also learned that some captives were held in facilities associated with UNRWA—the UN agency tasked with humanitarian aid—whose staff, in reality, took part in the

October 7 invasion and massacre.[10] This reflects a broader pattern of documented links between agency personnel and militant operations in Gaza.[11] One chilling example is Faisal Ali Mussalem al-Naami, an UNRWA social worker who was filmed loading the body of Yonatan Samerano into a vehicle to be abducted into Gaza.

It is clear to us that military pressure alone will not save the hostages and that the only way to free them is through a deal. But we do not know what will convince the kidnappers to agree to one. We understand, too, that every step we take from now will have fateful consequences. The hostages have no voice; we must be their voice. But how? And can anyone faithfully guide us?

Scrambling to chart a course of action, we consult with a host of people with experience in security, the military, diplomacy, and politics. The range of opinions is vast. Some insist categorically that campaigning for our loved ones' release is a mistake because only military action will get them out; others take the diametric view. This ambivalence will continue to haunt us, and we are often forced to make decisions based only on intuition and gut feeling.

Four days after we are discharged from the hospital, Friday night arrives, and we sit down in our Herzliya temporary home for a Shabbat meal, the first since we were abducted.

These moments, sitting at a table overflowing with plenty, remind me how Avshal and I used to cook Friday night feasts

---

10 United Nations, "UN Completes Investigation into Allegations of UNRWA Staff Involvement in October 7 Attacks," *UN News*, August 5, 2024, https://news.un.org/en/story/2024/08/1152841. (The investigation led to the termination of nine employees for their potential involvement).

11 "The Connection Between UNRWA and Hamas in Gaza," Israel National Digital Agency, accessed March 7, 2026, https://govextra.gov.il/unrwa/unrwa/.

in Be'eri. Our children and grandchildren joined us nearly every week, and Lilach and Tari often did too, along with other family members. We used to sit around a table covered with a festive tablecloth, a fresh challah under a special fabric cover in the center. Facing our chairs were plates and elegant silverware, which I inherited from my grandparents who fled to Israel from the Nazi regime.

We loved our family time so much, coming together to talk and argue, and of course watching the grandchildren chatter and play after dinner.

And again the realization strikes me. *None of that is coming back.* Neither Avshal nor the familiar dishes he made with his own hands. My throat tightens.

And within this emotional turmoil, I watch our grandchildren, each coping with the painful reality in their own way. Naveh is excited by the familiar faces around him, the many gifts, the fresh sense of freedom. The day after our release, he already understands that he can stop whispering. But Yula still whispers, even when she cries. It takes three weeks for her to begin speaking aloud again.

A few days later, Adi and I notice that Yula refuses to step out of the front door. We suddenly realize that she is still unsure whether the world outside is safe. In her mind, there are still terrorists roaming the streets, and any step outside could end with murder and bodies all around. It will take many more days of building trust before she internalizes that this new world is stable, that she can begin to let go of the fear that gripped her heart on October 7 and throughout captivity. We begin taking her outside gradually, first to the playground at the end of the street and later to the nearby beach.

The stream of visitors to our Herzliya temporary home does not stop. Family, friends, and acquaintances keep arriving to offer us comfort and help.

In the middle of the commotion, I get a call from Raz Ben Ami, a friend from Be'eri who was also abducted, in her case with her husband, Ohad. Ohad and I worked closely together on the kibbutz, and our relationship was always warm and respectful. Raz is released from Gaza two days after us, and I assume she wants to share her horrific ordeal, the ordeal that Ohad is still being forced to endure (thankfully, he will be released after 491 days in captivity). But to my surprise, she tells me that one of the terrorists who escorted her through the release process realized she was from Be'eri and asked her to send me his regards—and to tell my grandson Naveh that he misses him very much.

It turns out that a day before Raz was freed, her captors gathered all the hostages scheduled for the following day's release in the doctor's apartment where we were held for forty-three days. There they met the terrorists previously assigned to us, who were still responsible for the overall release process. I ask her what he looks like, and from her description, I immediately register: She is talking about Son Muhammad.

The surreal dissonance between the terrorists' unfathomable cruelty and their warm relationship with children strikes me again. This was the man who told me, "We are the same," *the same as the murderers,* and he misses Naveh. Words fail me to describe the whirlwind of emotion and the utter absurdity.

And I understand something else, too, something I had already suspected but is now reinforced. The four "Muhammads" who held us were senior Hamas operatives.

When I hang up—and I still cannot share parts of my conversation with Raz as the information is classified—I return to the garden, where everyone is still sitting and talking excitedly.

I understand that I must reduce my exposure to news about October 7 to an absolute minimum, at least for now, for the sake of my sanity and ability to keep functioning. What I saw with my own eyes was sufficiently monstrous that I cannot yet bear to hear what unfolded after we were already inside Gaza.

I ask everyone to spare me the detailed descriptions, and I try to drown out the snippets of information spoken around the table, although I know that in time, news of the horrors will reach me anyway, even if I try to avoid it.

One small mercy for now is that helps me for now is that my new phone has no WhatsApp history, sparing me the possibility of rereading the messages of terror I received from Lilach, my kibbutz friends, and acquaintances in Israel and around the world.

However, even though the terrorists looted my laptop, my Gmail account remains active, and with it, the past. When I find a few moments to myself, I scroll through the thousands of emails that poured in while I was held in Gaza, and only from the subject lines about Facebook posts by friends from Be'eri (I dare not click the links) do I begin to understand who from the kibbutz survived.

***

Three days after we walk free from Gaza, Yuval and Shaked tell us about what they did to bring us home. Yuval describes the massive march he organized, drawing in more than fifty thousand people despite the pouring rain. The march lasted five days over forty miles. It began on November 14, 2023, in a large plaza in Tel Aviv, which has since been renamed Hostages Square, and ended outside the Prime Minister's Office in Jerusalem. Along the way, Yuval called on decision-makers to treat the hostages as if they were their own children or siblings. "Show us that you are in control! Show us that you are taking responsibility for people who were simply sitting in their homes, celebrating the holiday. Bring them home! We don't know what condition they are in. We want them to hear our cry, and we want the Israeli public to join us and make its voice heard."

I look at the photographs and recognize Yuval at the front of the march, wearing a large straw hat, with photos of ten members of our family printed on his back: seven hostages, three murder victims.

I look at my son, such a shy and withdrawn individual until October 7, and I understand how the magnitude of the disaster forced him to grow in the heart of the storm, to rise above his natural instincts, and to become a grassroots leader who could lead tens of thousands behind him. And I am so proud of him.

I see the rivers of people marching for us, carrying the photos of the 255 hostages[12] and waving Israeli flags and yellow balloons. Yuval tells me about the food and drink stations organized along the route, about the generous hospitality awaiting anyone who chose to sleep along the way. The massive media coverage inspired hundreds of thousands more citizens to join the struggle.

All of this was happening while we were in Gaza, completely cut off from the outside world. Only now, as I write these lines,

---

12 During the October 7 massacre, 251 people were taken hostage into Gaza. The total number of hostages was 255 including the four individuals held there since before the war.

do I notice that this major march coincided with the date of my imaginary "open day" in Rwanda.

Shaked tells me that only two weeks after we were abducted, in her ninth month of pregnancy, she joined a delegation of hostage families that flew to meet members of the United States Congress in Washington, DC, despite the lack of insurance because of her advanced pregnancy. She describes running through the endless, long, labyrinthine corridors of Capitol Hill, repeatedly describing the cruelty of the Hamas terrorists who murdered her father, two of her uncles, and infants, children, women, and the elderly—the same terrorists who abducted her mother, sister, brother-in-law, and young niece and nephew. She told them about her fear that we were being held in inhumane conditions deep inside Gaza. In every meeting, she called on senior US officials: Do whatever you can to bring the hostages home. Only the release of all the hostages, she implored them, would allow the war to end and let Israelis and Gazans begin rebuilding.

She tells me about the creation of the Hostages and Missing Families Forum, which has become the hub of their collective activism. She also tells me about the huge mobilization of the Israeli public on behalf of the families affected by the massacre and about the massive donations from companies and individuals in Israel and around the world that have allowed the organization to operate.

Thanks to this determined activism, the hostages' cause remains at the top of the agenda on TV, in newspapers, and on social media. Graphic designers and marketing companies volunteer to create original symbols and slogans for the campaign. Posters with hostages' photos are draped over bridges, fences, and houses. Crowds wear shirts bearing the hostages' faces and cry, "Bring them home now!" Billboards and displays spread along Israel's main traffic routes and on major towers in the big cities; the hostages' faces loom next to a digital clock that marks the minutes, hours, and days that keep passing while they are still in Gaza. The call for the hostages' return is everywhere.

My younger brother, Aviv Havron, is the editor of the most influential weekend magazine in Israel, *Yedioth Ahronoth*. On October 27, while we were still in Gaza, he placed a photograph of little Yula on the front page: Just her alone, with text in his own handwriting calling for the return of this little girl and all the other hostages. This unusual step, taken by someone who has always insisted on staying behind the scenes, has a powerful impact as part of the struggle for the hostages and becomes etched in popular memory.

My kids and I hold a consultation about other ways to take action and conclude that as a released hostage, I must travel to New York and Washington to exert some influence on the US administration, House, and Senate.

My whole professional life, whether at major seed companies and later as the CEO of Fair Planet, I have been highly skilled at preparing for business trips. I have always owned tailored jackets and elegant pants, carefully paired suitcases that match my laptop bag, and countless travel accessories. I can finish packing in minutes, calculating the number of days and the kinds of events I will attend to maintain a suitable appearance for each meeting.

I remember the last time I packed my suitcase like this. It was October 6, the day before that despicable attack, when it never occurred to me that I might be forced to cancel my trip to the Netherlands for meetings with seed companies. And I realize that here, too, the loss is palpable. All the treasured clothes I collected over the years; my beautiful scarves from around world, from New York to Rome, from Paris to Pushkar, India; my boots and shoes; the jewelry I inherited from my grandmother and my mother… None of it exists anymore.

I scramble to get ready to fly. Since nearly every household in Israel will recognize my face (the footage of our release is being broadcast on a loop on television), I am nervous about shopping in ordinary stores. At a friend's suggestion, a professional stylist comes to fit me out with a respectable outfit, a thick coat, gloves, and a warm scarf because Washington is chilly in December. I pick a laptop bag and a suitcase from the La Palitte donation pile and fill it with essentials.

Shaked recommends that I fly with Einat Halevy Levin, whom she met on her previous trip to the United States. She is impressed with Einat's strategic grasp of international diplomacy and by her connections with high-profile members of Congress and senators. Scarcely two weeks after my release, on December 10, I board a plane with Einat to Washington, DC.

***

It is hard to describe the immense dissonance between the absolute helplessness of captivity and the experience of embarking on a new life mission as a free and autonomous individual, to campaign around the world for the freedom of my son-in-law Tal and all the other hostages. My body is still weak and fragile after our lengthy captivity, but my spirit is determined and focused.

I prepared for our meetings with a clear-eyed understanding of why these doors were opening. While my years of work with Fair Planet provided a professional context, I knew that the primary draw—the reason many in the US administration were so eager to meet me—was the raw human curiosity to see and hear a survivor of October 7 and Hamas captivity. I understand that I must take advantage of that curiosity to describe what really happened to us, to push the hostages to the top of the American agenda in particular and the global agenda in general, and to totally demolish Hamas' campaign of lies.

I have always known that humans are fundamentally limited in their ability to understand other people's experiences and feelings, and so the more personal a story is, the more identification it inspires, and with it, a willingness to act. I remember something Avshal used to tell me about his professional and business meetings: "Everything is personal." And I miss him so much.

To make Tal's presence felt in these meetings, as a kind of silent conversation partner, I bring two photographs of him and place them on the table in front of me. One of the pictures is a life-size photograph of his face smiling at the camera, radiating pure optimism and joy, his eyes shining brightly and a fashionable stubble framing his cheeks. In the second photo, he is lying on a soft white rug with his children nestled on top of him like two smiling blankets. A moment of blissful family life, so cruelly cut short.

Mere hours after we land in Washington, Einat and I are already running between meetings on Capitol Hill, and the doors swing open for us. Tal is a constant presence through his absence, and the photo of him with Naveh and Yula is gut-wrenching. Again and again, I describe what we endured and call on senior US officials to do everything to bring Tal and the other hostages home as soon as possible. In every meeting, I emphasize that the response of the United States and the international community to the events of October 7 and the abduction of hundreds of civilians from their homes is critical. Only a sweeping condemnation, followed up by effective action, can prevent the spread of the use of mass kidnapping as a new, simple, and horrifyingly cheap weapon of war. And in every meeting, I add that bringing the hostages home is the key to stopping the fighting, and I explain that only their return can make it possible for Gaza's civilian population to begin their own rehabilitation.

Our meetings with administration and congressional are initiated and facilitated by members of the American Jewish Committee (AJC), who mobilized immediately to help their brethren, their people. I meet many of them who lived quiet lives until the horrors of October 7 and whose Jewish identity was expressed mainly through their membership in a local community and neighborhood synagogue.

I was fortunate to live in the United States with Avshal and our three children for two years, in 1997–1999, after I received a Fulbright scholarship to do a postdoc in plant sciences at Rutgers University in New Jersey. Since then, I have felt that Jews in the Diaspora, especially in the United States, and the Jews in Israel have been living in two separate universes, aware of each other but disconnected.

The October 7 attack shook not only our lives, but theirs too. It is precisely Israel's weakness in protecting its own citizens, and specifically the existential threat to the Jewish people's only national home, that makes them grasp Israel's importance to their own security. I have never felt the connection between the Diaspora community and us, the Israelis, to be so powerful. Diaspora Jewry's existence depends on our existence, power, and independence in Israel, because they need to know that they can always pack up and move to Israel in any situation. And our own existence as Israelis depends on theirs, on their power in the Diaspora, on their influence in media and politics in their countries, and on their uncompromising support for us.

Flight follows flight, meeting follows meeting, and I find myself running around and acting in pursuit of my new life mission. In 2024, I fly eleven times to meet leaders, policymakers, intelligence officials, and influencers in the United States, France, Belgium, Austria, Spain, the Netherlands, and Rwanda. I also meet representatives of the Qatari embassies in Paris and Washington, and even the prime minister of Qatar during his visit to the US Congress.

In all these meetings, I ask that neither the fact that they took place nor any photograph be published. I am deeply fearful of Hamas monitoring my activity while Tal is still in their hands; any attention directed toward him could make Hamas raise its price for him in a deal and even endanger his life.

I am shaken by the refusal to condemn, in clear and unequivocal terms, the mass kidnapping of civilians from their homes and by the failure to understand that this is a new and devastating tactic that threatens global security no less than nuclear weapons, and yet it is easy and horrifyingly cheap to wield. It is clear to me that if the world fails to take decisive preventive measures, terrorist groups around the world will adopt this weapon of war.

More than anything, I am shocked by the failure to understand that freeing the hostages is the key to ending the fighting, to healing the Israeli people after the murderous attack of October 7, and to ending the suffering of civilians in the Gaza Strip.

I keep emphasizing that the international community's response to the October 7 hostage crisis is critical. And that only a full-throated condemnation, backed up by effective action, can prevent the spread of this toxic phenomenon.

I join the advisory board of Hostage Aid Worldwide, an organization that was founded by Nizar Zakka, a Lebanese Arab kidnapped in 2015 by Iran and unlawfully detained there for four years. After his release in 2019, he founded the organization to help hostages around the world and develop policy proposals to fight the scourge of these abductions.

In my first meeting with Nizar, I instinctively feel a connection with him. Only someone who has been a hostage, held captive, can understand—even without words—someone else who has endured a similar ordeal. Our cooperation, as an Arab Lebanese man and a Jewish Israeli woman, shows everyone who meets us that it is possible to work together in harmony, regardless of religion or national origin, toward a shared purpose.

On May 16, 2024, the US ambassador to the United Nations, Linda Thomas-Greenfield, invites me to testify before the UN Security Council (UNSC) about what happened to us on October 7 and in captivity. This is the first time I feel ready to appear in public, knowing my speech will be broadcast live and potentially seen by anyone in the world, including by Hamas.

Accompanied by Einat, I arrive at the UN headquarters in New York. We pass through security and enter the large plaza surrounding the tall main building. In the center is a large sculpture of a gun with its barrel tied in a knot, stopping it from firing. It is a symbol of peace, opposition to violence, and hope for a weapon-free future, and I think, *How far we are from that utopian vision.*

I look at the dozens of people crossing the plaza, hurriedly going about their business, dressed in elegant suits or cultural regalia, and I recall that until October 7, I was like them too, jetting around the world for work. I was on the strong side, supposedly invulnerable. Yet I am here, wearing a tailored jacket like them, but beneath this elegant exterior, I am a survivor of a terror attack, a survivor of Hamas captivity, walking free but wounded and shaken.

We are welcomed by representatives of the US Mission to the United Nations (USUN), who escort us to the large chamber where I will deliver my testimony. We enter a room packed to bursting with envoys of all fifteen Security Council member states, and I am asked to sit next to Ambassador Thomas-Greenfield, who initiated this session.

I am keenly aware that we are all, at our core, fundamentally alone in our experiences. I know that even if I describe everything we endured as directly, emotively, and clearly as possible, no one will ever be able to fully understand our suffering and distress. But my aim here, facing the most important international body in the world, is to do everything in my power to spur it to take action to secure the release of Tal and all the other hostages.

When it's my turn testify, I carefully consider every word and speak out of deep pain, but also conviction, to a silent chamber. I describe in impeccable detail the horrors of October 7, the terrible period of captivity with my daughter, small grandchildren, and other members of my family, the absolute deprivation of freedom, and the ever-present fear of death.

Occasionally, I lift my gaze to the national envoys listening. I recognize empathy, identification, and sometimes even tears on some of their faces.

And at the end of my remarks, I appeal to them and say:

> I come before you today, distinguished delegates, to ensure the safe release of Tal and all the other hostages; to ensure that both the released

and the current hostages receive the necessary support from the international community; to ensure that this never happens again. We cannot allow the normalization of this unprecedented form of terrorism: mass hostage-taking of unarmed civilians—women, children, elderly. What you see as *our* problem today might become a worldwide problem to each and every country in the near future.

Our hostages are victims of enforced disappearance, which the UN General Assembly stated in 2006 is a crime against humanity. No one knows better than me the tremendous risk of being a hostage. No one knows better than me the psychological distress caused by captivity. No one knows better than me that *every minute* counts. I call upon the UN Security Council to do everything in its power to prevent hostage taking from happening ever again. The UN Security Council should do everything in its power for the immediate and unconditional release of all the hostages. Bring them home now. My daughter and my little grandkids need their father, Tal Shoham, back home now.

And as a final note: If you care about the humanitarian situation in Gaza, like me, who dealt with humanitarian aid in all my professional life, use all the leverages and political power and do everything you can to bring all the hostages

> back home as soon as possible. Only this will enable the rehabilitation of the people in Gaza.[13]

After other October 7 survivors testify, the national envoys are invited to respond. Tense, I listen to the succession of statements, and at the end, we leave the UN building in the hope that our words will help to bring the crisis to an end. I fly back to Israel and count the hours, which turn into days, which turn into weeks, and the crisis remains without resolution.

---

13 "Dr. Shoshan Haran's Testimony in the United Nations About October 7th," posted May 20, 2024, by Noa Cohen-Orlov, YouTube, 10 min., 20 sec., https://www.youtube.com/watch?v=_EKChRGJ1zQ.

CHAPTER XIV
WRITING

Friday, November 8, 2024

IT HAS BEEN 346 DAYS since we walked free. Nearly a year. And Tal has been in captivity for 396 days. Thirteen months. Him and 146 other hostages. It is simply unimaginable.

In every mundane action, I think about Tal. Does he know day from night? Is he eating? Drinking? Being tortured? Showering? Shaving? What is his relationship with his captors like? Who is he with? When will he finally be released and reunited with Adi and his kids? With his parents? With us? When will we be able to breathe again?

It is absolutely clear to me that I cannot go back to living in Kibbutz Be'eri. With immense pain, I understand that I cannot live in the community my parents helped to establish, the place where I was born, where I grew up, got married, built a family, and lived for sixty-seven years of happiness.

I saw Be'eri with my own eyes as it was conquered, plundered, and trampled, its soil soaked with the blood of those I loved most. The trauma remains etched into every clod of earth, every stone, shrub, and tree. Within walking distance of the border, 120 of Be'eri's houses stand burned—a horrific realization of the vision drawn on those posters found in every Hamas household in Gaza. I know, perhaps better than anyone, the risks of living here.

I live now in a house in Nof Yam, a neighborhood of Herzliya, on one of its most charming streets. The road is lined with towering ficus trees on both sides, their trunks like massive elephant legs, tall canopies casting generous shade on the ground. But as beautiful as this place is, it feels bitterly foreign. I have been torn from my childhood vista, severed from my roots and the foundation of my life.

This spacious home was made available to us by a generous couple from England. When they heard from the neighbors what we had been through, they understood we needed temporary housing and immediately offered this house.

For the first few weeks, Adi, Naveh, and Yula live here with me. After they recuperate a little, they return to their family home in Galilee and to the supportive embrace of their community. On weekends they, and the rest of the immediate family, join me here until Saturday night.

And then the silence seizes control of the house again.

Every weekday morning, I open my eyes to a strange ceiling, wander alone through strange rooms, climb the stairs to the second floor alone, walk back down the stairs to the ground floor alone. Again and again and again. Alone. I am flooded with endless rage and cannot believe this is my life now.

I am homeless.

My beloved Avshal was murdered.

All my belongings, all our memories and our home, were looted and burned.

Saturday night, November 9, 2024

I look at tomorrow's calendar in dread. Nothing. All my meetings have been canceled or postponed. I have to do *something*. Something to hold me together. I am a woman in search of meaning.

For several weeks, I have been thinking about writing a book, but I feel gagged. Unable to write even a few sentences. Not even about Avshal. How can one begin to write about a man who was an entire world unto himself? Where does one start? How does one capture what he meant to others? And what he was to me? And more broadly: *How is it even possible that he is not here?*

I am facing a future without him, without the friend who offered such wise counsel and a boundless joy for life. I am left without our mutual respect and that braided independence we shared, a bond where we each drew strength from the other in a partnership of true equals.

I remember our dilemmas when we raised our children. Some were relatively minor decisions when they were in high school: Should we let them off the leash to get by independently, and if so, how much? Or should we always be there for them and solve every problem for them? And then when they were young adults, wondering what direction to take: Should we encourage them to follow their hearts or to take the track to greater financial security? Avshal and I each saw things a little differently, and together we laid out all the options for the children and left them with the freedom to choose. We always complemented each other, not through synthesis but by respecting our differences of approach and through mutual respect.

And I remember our late-night conversations about a dilemma we faced as I neared the end of my doctorate at the Robert H. Smith Faculty of Agriculture in Rehovot. As a family with three children in elementary school, could we relocate to the United States for two years so I could do a postdoc researching drug production from plants? Although it would advance my career, would Avshal's business career in Israel take a hit from his prolonged absence, and what would he do in the United States? How would the children get by in an environment so different from the kibbutz they knew? In the end, we decided that Avshal would take care of the children and the household so that I could focus on my research, although he later joined the Israeli Consulate General in New York as an accountant, and so this fascinating adventure ended up enriching all our lives with many wonderful experiences.

Avshal was a people person with a wide and diverse network of friends he picked up from every chapter in his life. Many of them confided in him, trusting his integrity, sensitivity, judgment, and ability to peer into their souls. He was a master at casting off routine and carving out slots of joy. He used to organize get-togethers with friends on the beach with a beer or at good restaurants, just for the heck of it, and countless trips for us across Israel and around the world.

All of this was cut off when he was murdered with unfathomable cruelty. And now he is missing from my life, missing from our children's lives, missing from the lives of the grandchildren he loved so much.

Grief washes over me. Grief over him, over me, over us. We will no longer complete the circle of life together.

I recall Picasso's *The Embrace*, from his Blue Period, which touched me profoundly. I saw it once at the Musée de l'Orangerie in Paris. It depicts a man and a woman locked in an embrace, leaning into one another for support. Each of them alone looks stricken with sorrow, limp and weak, but the leaning binds them into a strong, stable structure. Standing there in the gallery, I was struck by how Picasso managed to distill the strength of a loving relationship. Even in moments of the deepest sorrow, the painting conveys, leaning on one's spouse is a source of comfort, of steady support. It is a complete structure. And now I understand that I will never again be able to lean on Avshal like that. I will have to face whatever comes my way in the future without him, with only a gaping void in my life. This knowledge is too difficult to bear.

I keep thinking about his final moments, and the thoughts leave me no respite. What did he see? What did he do? What did he think? What did he feel? I try to skirt around these thoughts, to keep them locked away, but they keep flooding back. Here they come again. And again. And again.

***

Sunday, November 10, 2024

I wake to an empty day. I feel I must break the silence. Thoughts race through my mind, which feels like it is bursting at the seams. Flashbacks to what I saw and experienced on October 7, what I endured throughout fifty days of captivity in Gaza, that feeling of shock upon our return to Israel when we learned about the magnitude of the loss and the catastrophe.

Until today, I never thought I could face writing about this. It would be too painful. I have never written about personal things. I have only written professional scientific papers. I contemplate using a ghostwriter.

But this morning, I suddenly feel that perhaps writing will finally kickstart a process of coming to terms with what happened, communicating my story to the world. Perhaps others might draw strength from how I coped in captivity, much as books by Holocaust survivors steadied me when I was there.

The words bubble forth, in a level of detail that surprises even me, but I know that I have an even more urgent mission right now.

***

In mid-January 2025, Einat and I land at JFK in New York for the umpteenth time for another round of meetings scheduled with the help of the team at Hostage Aid Worldwide.

The goal: Keep applying pressure wherever possible and influence key figures in the incoming Trump administration to quickly advance a deal to bring the remaining hostages home.

We are on our way to Nizar and his wife Carol's home; our friendship with them has deepened in recent months. They have hosted us several times in their beautiful Washington house, where we now have our own bedrooms and know our way around the stunning nature paths surrounding their neighborhood. During the train ride, we start receiving reports of progress in the negotiations. An Israeli delegation has arrived in the Qatari capital of Doha, where senior Hamas figures are present, and now, so is President Biden's special envoy. We arrive at Nizar and Carol's home tired and exhausted.

At night I dream, for the first time, that Tal comes home, that he reunites with his children, that he is with Adi and with me. The dream is so real that I refuse to wake up. I try to hold on to every second of that blissful feeling of joy. I wake with a sense of hope. Tal is coming home. The moment is approaching.

That morning, a flurry of reports flies in: The deal is truly close to being sealed. It will reportedly be finalized in a day or two. I sit in front of the computer on Nizar's desk and do not know what to do with myself. The tension is unbearable. Every few seconds, I click "refresh" for an update.

It is hard to breathe.

CHAPTER XV
TAL WALKS FREE

15:39, Tuesday, February 18, 2025, Herzliya

SIXTEEN DAYS AFTER RETURNING FROM the US, I received a message from Adi Bershadsky, our liaison officer in the IDF: "Tal is scheduled to return this coming Saturday!" Finally, I could breathe again. Now, only three more days of tense anticipation remain. *I Just need them to pass so I can see him, watch him hugging Adi, his children, his parents and siblings...* I want to hug him myself.

Our nerves are frayed. The IDF Military Intelligence Directorate tells us to come on Saturday morning to Beilinson Hospital, where Tal will be airlifted after his release.

Saturday, February 22, 2025, Beilinson Hospital

09:15—We sit in a special room set aside for us and watch Al Jazeera's live broadcast from Rafah. The cameras pan across the stage prepared for the release ceremony, soaring past dozens of Hamas terrorists and hundreds of Gazan civilians who have crowded the square to watch. We wait in frenzied tension and suffocating dread. *When will Tal appear?* Will he look starved, his eyes rapt with horror and his cheeks sunken like my friends from Be'eri, Eli Sharabi and Ohad Ben Ami, when they were released from captivity two weeks earlier? Will he be paraded across the stage like a puppet on a string?

09:47—*There he is, that's Tal, walking onto the stage!* We erupt into colossal screams. Yuval leaps in the air with joy. Mor and Lee, Tal's siblings, burst into tears and embrace. He is thin, very thin, pale as chalk, blinking in the first daylight he has seen after many months held in the darkest tunnels.

But he is walking. On his own feet. Upright!

09:49—On the stage, flanking Tal, stand armed, masked Hamas terrorists in camouflage uniforms, green headbands across their foreheads, dressed exactly as they did when they released us. Tal grips the microphone handed to him by one of the terrorists and speaks, but we cannot hear him. A technical malfunction. Our stomachs turn. At least *he's* functioning!

Later, lip-reading experts decipher his words for me: "Thank you to the Qassam fighters who protected our security and our health." I remember the scripts the terrorists forced us to read in front of their video cameras at gunpoint, their weapons drawn, and I know they dictated his words too.

But who cares? Soon he will be rescued from their clutches.

09:52—Tal steps off the stage after the scripted ceremony and is loaded into a Red Cross vehicle. I breathe my first sigh of relief in 505 days.

At last, he is no longer a hostage.

10:12—Tal reaches the rendezvous with the Israeli army. When he steps out of the vehicle, still inside Gaza but in the hands of the IDF, they ask him if he needs anything. "Yes, the bathroom," he says. He enters the portable toilet, closes the door, makes sure nobody is watching, and performs a little dance.

10:27—Tal reaches Camp Re'im. He is in Israel. In a moment, he will reunite with his wife, his children, and his parents, all waiting there. He will hug them all with enormous emotion and walk holding Adi's hand on one side and Yula's on the other, with Naveh beside them. The tension in my body dissolves. I am engulfed in immense joy, mixed with exhaustion of surprising ferocity.

13:45—A helicopter descends toward the helipad at Beilinson Hospital. Tal steps out with his escorts and walks through a special corridor built to conceal him toward a black minibus with opaque windows. The minibus drives toward the hospital, but suddenly it stops, and the door flies open. Tal emerges, waving at the hundreds of people waiting to see him, a huge smile spread across his face.

Within minutes, he is in his own spacious hospital room, surrounded by his loved ones and every small thing denied to him in captivity. Even toothpicks, the first thing he asks to be brought.

When it is my turn to hug him, I feel mostly bones. But his eyes are gleaming, and he is completely focused. We do not speak much. Words are too insignificant to capture this moment.

And my ring, the one I left behind in Gaza, the one the terrorists promised to return with Tal, is not with him. Long after I returned to freedom, I learned they really did find the ring. They showed it to Yarden Roman-Gat, a hostage released from captivity a few days after us, and they told her too that they intended to return it with Tal. But later, it disappeared somewhere as they moved between hideouts and tunnels, between airstrikes and escape routes.

Sunday, February 23, 2025

09:03—Adi writes to me: "The kids fell asleep hugging Tal and started the morning with the words 'Mom and Dad.' *That's it. We made it.*"

I stare at the WhatsApp message on my phone and read it again and again and again. Her words flood me with happiness. Adi, who survived the horrific ordeal of captivity with me and her children, is finally reunited with Tal. The four of them can breathe fresh air again together. Tal has come home. To them. To our extended family. And to everyone in this country who has stood with us and campaigned without pause for the hostages' release.

The day after Tal returns, he meets Aviv's younger daughter, Ella, and tells her, "I saw you on television in Gaza, holding a sign at a protest with my photo. It gave me so much strength." They hug and cry.

Many other returning hostages describe how they drew strength and hope in captivity when caught glimpses of the rallies and interviews calling for their release. And I cast my mind back to all those who opposed the hostages' families' demonstrations and pressured them to stay quiet, claiming that they were serving Hamas. It is clear to me this advice was mistaken and quite possibly intended to achieve other goals instead.

Only weeks after Tal is released is he able to start talking, in piecemeal fashion, about what he endured. In small moments of free time away from the children, away from his new life, he describes what he experienced over the course of 505 days: One year and four and a half months of hell.

Only then do I learn the horrific details of those final dramatic moments in the safe room and Avshal's last words to him.

"We heard gunfire and glass smashing," Tal recalls, "and we realized the terrorists had broken into the house. Avshal and I held the table extensions and pressed them against the handle of the safe room door so they couldn't break in. The terrorists placed explosives on the handle mechanism and blew it up. The screws flew into the safe room; they looked like bullets. When we understood there was no way out and we couldn't escape, Avshal patted me on the shoulder and said, sarcastically, 'It's been a pleasure.' He already reckoned it was all over for him."

I listen to Tal and a shiver ripples through my body. This is the first time I am hearing what my beloved husband's final words were, minutes before he was murdered. Maybe those few words, effectively summing up his life as the inferno raged around us, offer some measure of solace. For me. For us. *"It was a pleasure."* Avshal was a man who knew how to enjoy life, to seize the moment. He also had an instinctive ability to read the room, to pick up on nuances. And he understood. For him, it was over.

And there I was, sprawled on the cold safe room floor, repressing reality, refusing to believe this was happening to us. My mind was frozen. I missed his final words.

In those seconds, Tal told himself, "It's not over till it's over. I'm going to fight until the last moment." But a few minutes later, we heard the screeching of a bulldozer's bucket. The terrorists smashed into the safe room window. Avshal lunged toward the window, and when the bulldozer pulled back, he slammed it shut again and tried to lock it, but the bulldozer struck again until it ripped open a crack that let them throw a grenade inside. For a few seconds, the terrorists made eye contact with Tal and Avshal. They raised their hands to surrender while Tal shouted that there were children in the safe room. Tal was yanked out through the window, and Avshal after him. After that, Tal never saw Avshal again and did not know what became of him.

We have to break that horrible news to him now....

Tal was led around three hundred feet into the kibbutz. He saw the terrorists standing in the middle of the road, laughing at him, filming him for TikTok or Instagram. He also saw bodies, people executed with a gunshot to the head. They had not been shot in the back while trying to run away; they had been pressed down and were shot point blank.

The terrorists shoved Tal into a car trunk, with three more hostages from Be'eri already inside: Yarden and Alon Gat with their daughter, Gefen.

Alon Gat fills in the details about what happened while Tal was lying in the trunk. "I try to tell Tal we're in a car and to describe what was happening around us, but then the three terrorists in the front start getting very aggressive, and I have to stop talking. A few hundred feet from the border fence, the terrorists spot an IDF tank, stop the car, and run to hide among trees."

Alon and Yarden seized the opportunity, jumped out with Gefen, and ran toward a nearby IDF post. When they reached it, they discovered it was abandoned. Then the terrorists noticed them and started chasing and firing at them. Yarden passed Gefen into Alon's arms, and as they ran and tried to take cover, they split up. Yarden's strength failed her; she fell to the ground and played dead, but the terrorists saw her, grabbed her by the arms, and dragged her back to the vehicle. Alon kept running with Gefen in his arms and managed to evade pursuit. For close to twenty-four hours, they hid inside a thicket as they heard terrorists prowling around them. The next morning, they fled back to Kibbutz Be'eri and to freedom.

But Yarden was kidnapped into Gaza, and when she was hauled out of the car, she was displayed as a trophy before hundreds of cheering Palestinians. That was how she described it after she was released in the same deal that also brought us back to Israel.

As a crowd of Gazans swarmed around Yarden, the terrorists hauled Tal from the trunk. In those chilling moments, one of the gunmen leapt onto the roof of the car and pointed his weapon at Tal at point-blank range. With murder in his eyes, he barked an order to kneel. Tal resolved right then that he would not give them the satisfaction of seeing him afraid. As the terrorist continued to scream, Tal's mind went elsewhere, focused and cold. *I don't get to decide if he kills me*, he thought, *but if he does, it's on my terms.* Instinctively, he raised his hands and looks his would-be executioner in the eye. "I surrender," he said firmly. "There is no reason to kill me." They remained in that standoff for a grueling thirty seconds before another terrorist arrived, grabbed Tal by the shoulder, and began marching him through the streets of Gaza.

And I ask myself, *How would I have behaved in such a situation*? Would I have knelt at gunpoint, or would I have refused that humiliation? But the most fateful decisions, I know, are made in a split second. Will they point us to life or death? No one knows how they would act in such extreme circumstances.

And *perhaps*, a thought comes to mind, *perhaps* the way we might react depends on whether we are alone, left to our own devices, or with people we love. Perhaps when you are by yourself, focused only on the "here and now," and no one else's life depends on you in that moment, you can react differently.

I will never know.

They took Tal to a town in Gaza, put him on a motorcycle, and filmed him in the streets for about half an hour. The terrorists were shouting, "Jewish soldier! Pig!" People in the street tried to get their hands on him, to hit him with sticks or punch him, to curse and spit at him. It was crystal clear they were overjoyed with what Hamas' terrorists has done. Luckily the driver kept moving, or they probably would have beaten him to death. In the end, they took him to a house that he later understood belonged to a senior Hamas figure.

The kidnappers told Tal that the house was in northern Gaza. He was held there for several weeks under strict guard, handcuffed, alone. "From the start, I decided I would demand respect and human treatment from my captors. I didn't lower my gaze. I stood upright and looked them in the eye. I also decided to speak to them like human beings, even though they were terrorists who had just committed atrocities. I didn't care about that in the moment."

In those early days, the terrorists did not even let Tal walk around the room. They wanted him to sit or lie down all day, but he tried to pace around without them seeing because that was the only way he could think clearly.

To humanize himself in his captors' eyes, and in the hope of reducing his chances of getting murdered, Tal drew on the Arabic he had learned in school. He managed to improve his fluency during his time in captivity, using the language to speak with his captors about life in Israel. Sometimes they asked him to translate Israeli radio broadcasts into Arabic for them. That was how he learned about the magnitude of the horrors of October 7. "On one station, they interviewed a ZAKA volunteer," he says, referring to the volunteer search and rescue agency. "In tears, he described what he saw in Be'eri, and I thought to myself: *How bad could it have been?* So he saw some mangled body parts, is that a reason to start bawling? Only later did I learn the ISIS-style horrors they committed in Be'eri, things I'd rather I never knew."

The terrorists, for their part, were euphoric and boasted about their massacre of innocents.

One of the first things that shocked Tal in the Gaza apartment was the terrorists' utter disregard for their own people's lives. They brandished a remote control and warned him that if he attempted to escape, they would detonate the entire building. "I'm not planning to escape," Tal replied, but hearing the muffled voices of women and children through the walls, he asked them anyway, "But what about the neighbors?"

Their answer was chillingly nonchalant: "They'll die and become *shahids*. We don't care."

That answer rattled him. He understood that Hamas did not care about Palestinian civilians in Gaza and had no misgivings about using mosques and ambulances as cover for terrorism. By way of illustration, Tal recalls that when he was moved from the hideout to the tunnels, the captors shoved him into a Red Crescent ambulance, where Hamas terrorists were already waiting inside.

Ahead of his release, they took him to a mosque where at least ten armed terrorists had turned the house of worship into a command base. The experience taught him that Hamas would exploit every means at its disposal, as a matter of malicious strategy, to make it harder for Israel to fight back; they were even willing to sacrifice the lives of Palestinian civilians in order to flaunt their deaths for propaganda.

It is only after his release that Tal is confronted with the CCTV footage from October 7. He watches as thousands of

Gazan civilians flood into Israeli communities—looting, destroying, and even stealing the bodies of the murdered. He sees what has already become a symbol of this betrayal: The involvement of UNRWA staff, including the video of an agency employee dragging a body from Be'eri and loading it onto a vehicle bound for Gaza.

Whenever the terrorists feared that Israeli forces were closing in on the hostages' location, they moved them to a new hideout. These transfers often took place during curfews, when Gazan civilians were confined to their homes. On one occasion, they disguised Tal as a woman, completely shrouded in a veil, allowing them to slip through the crowds undetected.

In one of the apartments that he was taken to, the terrorists brought two more hostages: Evyatar David and Guy Gilboa-Dalal, young men who had been kidnapped from the Nova Festival. Tal spent most of his captivity with them from that point on. Over the many months they were forced to spend together, Evyatar and Guy told him how in their first two weeks in captivity, they were both shackled, hands and feet, hands cuffed behind their backs, black sacks over their heads, faces pressed against the wall. Guy recalled that the thirst had been so severe that when the terrorists allowed him to go to the bathroom and looked away for a moment, he dunked his head into a bucket of filthy water meant to be used for flushing the toilet, just to be able to drink *something*.

Evyatar and Guy told him that they had been beaten daily. They told him that the terrorists had mocked them, made gunfire sounds, and kept asking them how the party was—the party they were kidnapped from. Their horrific ordeal made Tal feel lucky about the way he had been treated. Relatively speaking, of course.

As I listen, it dawns on me that I will never truly comprehend what Evyatar, Guy, and Tal went through. Only someone who has endured similar torture might understand.

Their hunger was so extreme that it woke them up at night, and the psychological torment was so intense, they sometimes feared they would not survive the night. Early on, they were very, very, very scared—practically certain—that the terrorists would execute them at night. Tal retreated into himself, prompting Guy and Evyatar to ask what he was he doing, Tal answered, "I'm *saying goodbye to life.*" He wanted to be in a place where if this was really the end, then at least he was going without regrets or guilty feelings.

But for Tal, the most agonizing torture was the uncertainty about his family. He spent all day thinking, *Are they still alive? Are they dead?* He tried to imagine what it would be like to be released and reunited with one of them, with two, or with none. About a month into captivity, he imagined himself burying them, one big grave and two little ones, with his whole community behind him, as he delivered a eulogy for them. It was the hardest thing he had ever done.

And then, some three weeks later, Tal received an earth-shattering piece of news. His captors brought him the letter that Adi had written him the day before we were released. The terrorist who handed it to him, the same one who came to visit our captors, threatened him that if he told anyone, they'd kill him.

Tal gripped the page with Adi's handwritten note, in English, describing how she and the children had been kidnapped together with me, Sharon, and Noam, that we were OK, that Naveh and Yahel were managing to cope in captivity, and that they were all about to be released soon. When he finished reading, his whole body healed at once, and all the tension flooded away.

He started glowing from inside with happiness. He went to Guy and Evyatar and said, "*Adi and the kids are alive!* Please excuse me as I start crying under the blanket." For half an hour, he released all the tears he had been holding inside, but out of gratitude and joy. It was the first time he had cried in Gaza. Now that the weight of his family was off him, he could focus on his own survival. He knew that the terrorists would not break him. That his kids were going to get their daddy back.

One day, when the hostages were forced to switch hideouts again, they were taken to a house that we recognized from Tal's description; it was the same house where we were held for one night—night six: the "Hello Kitty house." Another terrorist squad was waiting for them there. One of them suddenly asked, "Who is Abu Naveh? Which one of you is Naveh's dad?"

Tal was stunned when the terrorist told him he was on the team that had guarded us for fifty days. He brought Tal a light blue sheet that Naveh had slept on and mentioned that Yula used to joke around with them. He even showed Tal a little prank she taught him in Hebrew: The terrorist would say "*Ma?*" (*What?*) and she would squeal, "*Tapuach adama!*" (*Potato!*).

Tal became deeply depressed at the thought of missing such meaningful moments in his children's development. It haunted him that the terrorists—the people who had kidnapped them!—got to experience those moments instead of him.

Even after Adi and the children were released, the terrorists continued to torment them psychologically. They sent Adi text messages threatening to kill Tal or claiming he had already been murdered. She received a call from someone speaking Hebrew with a heavy Arabic accent, warning her that if she said a single word about her conditions in Gaza, they would murder him.

For long stretches of time, Tal and his fellow hostages suffered extreme starvation, especially early in their captivity and toward the end. The captors gave them only one pita a day or a small portion of rice; they were hungry and thirsty all the time. The hunger made his stomach hurt so badly that he cannot even describe the pain. The hostages begged their captors—even agreeing to give them massages just to get more food—while their captors stayed in their own air-conditioned room with plenty to eat.

By October 2024, after months in the tunnels, the hostages' physical condition was deteriorating so severely that every time Tal stood up, he felt as though a black scarf was being pulled over his eyes. To stop himself from fainting, he had to lean against the cold wall for twenty or thirty seconds, waiting for the world to stop spinning. Even a ten-minute walk around the cramped room required a monumental effort, yet the three men forced themselves to do it, a desperate ritual to keep their bodies from giving up.

Tal's limbs became swollen. It started with a blue mark on his leg, and then the whole leg became a kaleidoscope of blue, purple, and yellow. For over a month, he could not walk. The pain became unbearable to the point that he could not even move. He developed scurvy, a disease that hardly exists anymore in the developed world. It is caused by malnutrition and a severe deficiency of Vitamin C. The body simply starts breaking itself down from the inside.

I am completely taken aback to hear Tal describing the moments of spirituality he found in captivity and the efforts that he and his fellow hostages made to maintain Jewish traditions in the heart of Gaza.

"Every Friday night, we performed a Kabbalat Shabbat ritual to welcome the Sabbath," he recalls. "We tried to observe the holidays too, but we didn't always know when they fell. We could always count the days to Shabbat, but the festivals were harder. The terrorists deliberately gave us the wrong dates to throw us off—they were trying to break us mentally. They shouted at us and sometimes spit on us as we tried to pray."

He reflects on the necessity of clinging to their Judaism in captivity: "Being a hostage in Gaza is a twisted reality, it's hard to describe to anyone who wasn't there. But practicing just a few traditions was what helped us maintain our sanity and identity. It gave us a sense of strength and comfort."

Later, they would need truly superhuman strength to survive even more horrific conditions. In June 2024, the captors promised Tal that he would be moved to a "doctor's house" in the northern Gaza Strip, promising electricity, food, and clean water. Desperate for hope, he wanted to believe them.

The hostages were led down the street in broad daylight, disguised as Palestinians among the local population. A Red Crescent ambulance arrived, manned by armed terrorists. After a twenty-five-minute drive, the vehicle stopped. The hostages were blindfolded and led on foot across sandy terrain. They walked for hours between unseen walls until Tal realized the air had grown thin. They had entered a tunnel.

Deep inside, Tal, Evyatar, and Guy met Omer Wenkert, another hostage who had survived 197 days alone in the dark. "As we crossed the threshold, the guards told him, 'We've brought you some friends,'" Tal recounts. "That was when I knew. I understood right then that we were going to be in that tunnel until the end."

The four men were confined to a space roughly three feet wide and thirty-three feet long. One end was a wall, the other an iron door. They were held a hundred feet underground with no air circulation or natural light. Their only "comforts" were four mattresses on a sandy floor and a pit for a toilet.

The captors used light as a weapon. Three small bulbs provided a relentless, artificial glare that shattered their internal sense of time. Then, without warning, the terrorists would cut the power, plunging them into a blackness so absolute they could not see their own hands. After several such "blackouts," the truth became clear: This was no technical failure, it was deliberate torture.

The oxygen levels were so depleted that it took Tal three weeks just to clear the brain fog. They slept fourteen hours a day, their bodies shutting down from hypoxia. They barely spoke.

Their captors viewed them as less than human, torturing them for sport. Sometimes they ignited scraps of paper or rubber specifically to consume the remaining oxygen. As smoke filled the room, the hostages were forced to lie on the floor, gasping for air. At one point, one of Tal's fellow hostages took his hand and whispered, "I need you to hold me, I'm losing it."

Tal replied, "Take a deep breath. We can still breathe. This isn't over." Yet, in his heart, Tal suspected they would all suffocate within the hour.

The conditions were stifling. Humidity reached unbearable levels; their clothes, perpetually soaked with sweat, clung to them like a second layer of filth. Despite the heat, they were forbidden from removing their shirts. Cameras monitored them twenty-four hours a day. At times, the captors prohibited sleep, monitoring the feed to ensure total obedience; any lapse meant their meager rations were cut further.

"They let us shower and change once every twenty-one days," Tal says. "Most of the time we were dirty and stinking, our only company were the fruit flies and a mouse. Every two weeks, the terrorists would spray pesticide to kill the flies, and, as if by accident, they would spray us with the chemicals too. They enjoyed doing it specifically after they let us shower."

The mental cruelty was relentless. The terrorists would force the four men to choose which of them would be murdered first. They threatened to blow up the tunnel if the IDF approached. "I wondered every day if I would wake up," Tal admits. "I was afraid. I didn't want to die. But the conditions were so horrific that sometimes I thought there was something soft and calm in death—in finally accepting that it could happen at any moment."

For eight and a half months, Tal survived by focusing on what he could control: his inner life. He practiced mindfulness—a technique he learned from Adi, a psychologist. He opened up to the others, and together they devised rituals to remember their humanity. At the end of every day, they made a habit of discussing their disagreements and airing tensions so they could fall asleep on good terms. In that airless dark, they became a single unit. A family.

On January 21, 2025, one of the captors told the four men that a deal had been struck for the release of hostages. But he immediately followed it up with a gut-wrenching clincher: "There will be good news for two of you, and bad news for the other two. You'll find out tomorrow."

The next day, the guard returned with a camera to record their reactions, exploiting their raw anxiety for propaganda. For the next two and a half weeks—which felt like an eternity—the terrorists toyed with them, playing malicious mind games: "Maybe you're getting out…no, wait, maybe it's that other guy."

Early in the morning of February 18, Tal and his friends were awoken and taken to the terrorists' own quarters for the first time. The captors filmed the men receiving a large plate of rice and meat—a staged performance intended to deceive the world into thinking they were well-fed. There, the commander told Tal he was being released alongside Omer Wenkert. Guy and Evyatar would remain behind.

For Tal, the joy of freedom was poisoned by the weight of those he was leaving. As the eldest, he had served as a buffer between the younger men and their captors, often intervening to de-escalate tricky situations or shield them from beatings. He was terrified for their lives, fearing they wouldn't know how to endure the isolation without him. He tried to urge them to keep fighting, but as the hours ticked down, he saw them simply falling apart. Finally, they were separated. Omer and Tal were led out of the tunnel.

Reflecting on his first moments above ground, Tal says, "I took a deep breath and felt the dew on my skin. It felt incredible to inhale fresh oxygen again—to breathe in the clean air after the rain. It was an uplifting, almost holy experience."

Tal was moved to a house in Rafah equipped with electricity, a shower, and plenty of food. He knew they were fattening him up for the cameras. "It wasn't until Friday night," he recalls, "when I saw my name and photo published and heard a Hamas spokesman confirm the list, that I knew for sure I was going home."

On February 22, 2025, Tal's journey home was broadcast to millions of people around the world. In a bizarre, public ceremony in Nuseirat, Omer Wenkert and two other hostages were displayed before their final release. But the terrorists' cruelty had one final layer: They forced Guy and Evyatar to watch the ceremony from inside a vehicle with the door left open. Hamas later released a video of them in those moments, begging to be freed. Tal is haunted by that image. "It was shattering to see someone who was with me for 250 days left behind, not knowing their fate, while we were released," he says.

Tal made a solemn vow that day. Interview after interview, speech after speech, he and Adi campaigned tirelessly for Guy, Evyatar, and the remaining captives, sacrificing their own recovery time to ensure no one was forgotten.

On October 13, 2025—after 738 days—the miracle finally happened. All living hostages returned to Israel. The country was flooded with a tidal wave of emotion. I have barely turned on my television since my own release, but even I found myself watching the live broadcasts all day, swept up in the exhilaration of the reunions.

Tal was finally reunited with Guy and Evyatar at Beilinson Hospital. He gave Evyatar a long, silent embrace, then walked into Guy's room. Guy was asleep. "Guychuk, it's time to wake up," Tal whispered, stroking his head just as he had done so many times in the darkness of the tunnel.

Guy pulled off his sleep mask, blinking as he processed the surprise. A slow smile spread across his face. "Dude," he replied, "I love that you're waking me up again. Wow."

"So do I," Tal agreed.

PART 3
RESOLVE

CHAPTER XVI

BRAINWASHING

SOME MONTHS AFTER OUR RELEASE, my family and friends finally tell me that on the morning of October 7, even before 7:00 a.m., Hamas launched a choreographed social media campaign claiming that Israel was committing "genocide" in Gaza. This absurd campaign went live at the exact moment the terrorists started murdering, raping, and kidnapping children, women, and men. As we were attacked, defenseless, they were already brainwashing the world.

The revelation stuns me and fills me with rage and frustration. I check whether it is really true. I learn that the Israeli journalist Guy Rolnik, who has investigated the impact of social media networks, reported on the issue in a series of investigative reports that aired on Israeli television in January 2024—A Network of Mass Destruction.[14] He gathered evidence of how Hamas prepared, alongside the massacre, to launch a sophisticated assault to turn global public opinion against Israel, long

---

[14] Rolnik, G. (2024, January 21) [Video]. Kan 11. https://www.kan.org.il/content/kan/kan-11/p-685602/s1/688258/

before the IDF even entered Gaza in response to Hamas' murderous invasion.

I decide to watch Rolnik's documentary series. I turn on the television, dormant ever since I moved into this temporary home. I cannot bear to watch the news, the endless panel shows, or the entertainment programs that keep rolling as if October 7 never happened, and I find the first episode of the series. Almost immediately, I feel a surge of rage, frustration, and grief, and I switch the television back off. I realize that in my current state, I have tolerance only for the written word; the images of the horrors unleashed on us are too much.

I search and find the reports in print[15].

Rolnik's analysis reveals that the events of October 7 in Israel were unprecedented in human history, but not because of the scale of the atrocities. History is littered with horrific events: Pogroms and the Holocaust, the Armenian genocide, the massacre of the Rohingya in Myanmar, mass killings in Africa, ISIS' sadistic violence, the 9/11 attack. The October 7 Massacre, however, was a historic turning point because of another, follow-up terror attack, this one digital, that went practically unchallenged for a long time.

This was a two-pronged attack. The first was a claim of Palestinian victimhood, the charge that "Israel is committing genocide against us." The second was the amplification of Hamas' own atrocities.

The terrorists used multiple platforms to broadcast their atrocities. They exploited the victims' own phones to launch Facebook Live streams, forcing families to witness the murder or

---

15 Lavi, A. (2024, January 19). *Interview with Guy Rolnik: "Hamas started a huge campaign against us on social media while they were still massacring our people"* [In Hebrew]. Zman Yisrael.

kidnapping of their loved ones in real time. Simultaneously, they distributed GoPro bodycam footage through Telegram. In some of the most diabolical instances, they spliced raw phone footage with recorded moments of the killings to create gruesome, edited propaganda designed to inflict maximum psychological terror.

Hamas' terrorists understood that on the physical battlefield, they could hurt thousands of people, but in the battlefield over the global consciousness, they could strike ten million Israelis, four hundred million viewers in the Middle East, and the whole world. These tools might be even more powerful than a rifle.

And that was just the first visible wave. It coincided with another far-reaching, lavishly funded assault that leveraged precision targeting tools on social media to inflame whole societies, all around the world, using personally tailored propaganda spread with the help of a vast army of bots, avatars, and "sock puppets" (fictional accounts). When all these digital tools were activated to attack Israel and Jews at once, they quickly swept up millions of people, most of whom had never considered this conflict but went along with the zeitgeist without realizing it had been engineered by Hamas and its supporters.

Rolnik concludes that the internet giants knew what was happening and chose to stay silent—and rake in enormous profits from the traffic.

One day, as I drive to my weekly therapist's appointment, I listen to Yuval Weinreb's podcast *Getting to Know China*, a vast country whose culture has always fascinated me. In this episode[16], Yuval interviews Barak Herscowitz, a former employee at TikTok, a Chinese company, who spills the beans about what

---

[16] Weinreb, Y. (Host). (n.d.). Episode 136: Barak Hershkowitz on TikTok's scandalous conduct after October 7th [Audio podcast episode]. In Getting to Know China.

happened inside the company after October 7. I listen and my anger rises.

Barak says that on October 9, a Monday, the first day of the working week at TikTok after the attack, he saw how the popular platform's algorithms were shaping young minds worldwide. He started monitoring and making records of the problematic posts and discovered a clear bias in favor of extreme anti-Israel positions and Iran-backed terror groups. Meanwhile, he was reading the internal correspondence of employees on TikTok's Trust and Safety team and discovered they were blocking posts that expressed shock at the attack on Israel.

He noticed that even content about us, hostages held at gunpoint by Hamas, even photos of us with the caption "Kidnapped to Gaza," was blocked by Trust and Safety on the bizarre pretext that this was "political content."

Shocked and furious, Barak wrote a detailed internal memo warning TikTok executives about the severe bias. They chose to ignore him, and he resigned. In time, the memo made its way to a US Senate hearing and the international media, exposing the tip of the iceberg of a psyops campaign to undermine Israel's international legitimacy, even its right to exist, as well as the spread of antisemitic content, and the information warfare waged by hostile states and other anti-Western actors—a battleground on which the democratic world is, for now at least, on the losing side.

The deluge of lies across digital media landed on the fertile soil of anti-Semitism, silent yet latent, which quickly became a tsunami of anti-Israel and anti-Jewish hatred online. Like a germ that latches onto a juicy piece of food and multiplies exponentially until it takes over the entire object. That is exactly how I used to demonstrate it to my students in the microbiology lab:

We would open Petri dishes filled with a sterile, bacteria-friendly foodstuff, close them after a few minutes, and then twenty-four hours later, we would see how every dish was covered in trillions of bacteria that had multiplied overnight.

As I drive alone to the cemetery in Omer for the memorial marking two years since my beloved Avshal's murder, I listen to a firsthand account of how this campaign of lies spread at a dizzying speed to shape the minds and behavior of students in the United States. On the radio is an interview by the journalist Roni Kuban with Maya Tevet Dayan, a visiting professor of poetry at the University of San Diego.

Maya says that as early as October 10, 2023, her entire campus was covered with pro-Palestinian stickers. I break into a cold sweat and immediately calculate: October 7 was a Saturday, October 8 was a Sunday…Americans were on their weekend… but that means that on October 9, the first workday after we were attacked, someone designed the stickers, got them printed, brought them to the university, and recruited people to distribute them, so that by the next morning, they were already plastered all over campus.

I sink into even deeper shock when I hear Maya say that the same morning, the doors of Jewish students' dorm rooms were daubed with stars of David, and from that moment, not a single Jewish student came to class. Fear had driven them into hiding, into staying at home.

When Maya insisted on continuing to teach her course, she was forced to go underground, teaching in a different classroom each time, notifying students of the location only ten minutes before each class began, so that the pro-Palestinian students would not have a chance to disrupt the lesson.

Stunned by this explosion of anti-Semitism, Maya tried to get her head around what is happening. She invited one of her students, a young woman from the Netherlands, for a conversation and the student told her bluntly, "I'll try to explain, but this goes way back. It's something we grew up with, in our jokes, in our conversations around the dinner table. We just don't like Jews."

Maya asked her, "Who is *we*?"

The student answered, "I grew up in the Netherlands. We, my family, don't like you. I can like you personally. We don't like Jews, and most of the time, we have to say that quietly. Now we're allowed to say it out loud. It's a very, very deep sentiment, no matter what the academic analysis or articles about anti-Semitism are telling you."

That conversation breaks Maya's heart.

Personally, I came to understand the ancient roots of anti-Semitism many years earlier, when I read *The Pity of It All: A Portrait of Jews In Germany 1743-1933* by Amos Elon. The book opens with an account of Moses Mendelssohn, then aged fourteen, entering Berlin in 1743 through the gate for Jews and livestock. At the time, Jews were forbidden from entering the city through the regular human gate. This was the same Mendelssohn who would, in time, become one of the world's most respected and famous philosophers.

At the end of the book, Elon describes the Jewish philosopher Hannah Arendt's escape from Germany in 1933, after the Nazis, whose rise to power was profoundly rooted in German anti-Semitism, stripped her of her citizenship.

That same year, my own grandparents, Edgar and Aanna Heilbronner also fled Nazi Germany after their medical licenses were revoked because they were Jews. After an arduous journey, they reached Jerusalem with their small children: Laura (Shoshana), who would die of cancer at fourteen, after whom I am named; Gerhard (Abraham), my father[17]; and Hans (Hanan). That was how they escaped getting murdered in the extermination camps. And that was how my life—and my family's lives—became a possibility at all.

The Pity of It All describes how German Jewry flourished culturally, economically, and socially for almost two hundred years, producing some of the world's most prominent personalities in the humanities, sciences, and arts, including Albert Einstein, Sigmund Freud, and Franz Kafka.

Yet this brief renaissance between when Jews had to enter Berlin through the gate reserved for livestock and their industrial extermination in the Holocaust illustrates how anti-Semitism never disappeared. It festered above and beneath the surface, waiting to erupt again with explosive force when the Nazis rose to power.

In the cataclysmic aftermath of the Second World War and Holocaust, there were attempts to curb anti-Semitism through government policy and laws, but beneath this slender veneer lay the same fertile soil in which Hamas' psyops campaign struck its roots, precisely as its men committed mass atrocities on October 7—the deadliest day for the Jewish People since the Holocaust.

***

During one of my trips to the United States as part of the campaign to bring the hostages home, I encounter a phenomenon that I cannot quite define at the time. When I meet

[17] Following his marriage to my mother, Rina, in 1952, my father Hebraized his surname, changing it from Heilbronner to Havron.

self-identifying progressive Jews, I feel that some of them—a minority, admittedly—treat me with a certain hostility, if only through their body language and looks, although not verbally. It is profoundly hurtful.

Me? I was kidnapped by terrorists into Gaza with my daughter and tender grandchildren. *Me?* My husband was murdered. So were my sister and more than one hundred of my friends from Kibbutz Be'eri. *Me?* My home was burned down, leaving me homeless and destitute. I receive not even a drop of sympathy from these Jews—my own people, whose hearts are meant to bleed, or so they imagine themselves, for the weak and downtrodden. To my astonishment, I understand that their sympathy is reserved for Palestinians only.

What I grasp in these (thankfully rare) moments is that these people are in deep denial. They refuse to confront the truth of what happened, even when it was caught on camera, closing their eyes to anything that doesn't match their own carefully constructed view of the world. Absurdly, my mere survival through the massacre and Hamas captivity, my physical presence near them, embodying and bearing witness to the horrors I endured, threatens to upend their worldview. In the most surreal way, it is like meeting me offends *them*.

It takes me a long time to recover from the shock of those encounters.

Only many months later do I understand the deeper reason for this disturbing phenomenon. Whether out of ignorance or an inability to think, out of credulity in the face of Hamas' lies or just plain condescension, these people look at the people of Gaza as helpless, wretched refugees. They strip them of agency and thus absolve them of responsibility for their own actions.

For brutal acts of murder, mass kidnappings, sexual violence[18], and sheer depredation.

During an intimate gathering in New York, when I speak about my friend Vivian Silver, who founded Women Wage Peace and was murdered on October 7, I hear a sentence that distils this perfectly. One of the participants says to me, "We were not fast enough to bring peace," referring to herself and Vivian.

What a twisted understanding! As if it was all the fault of peace activists in Israel and West Bank, in New York or anywhere in that world, for having failed to bring peace, and that is why the massacre happened. Hidden in her words was the belief that Hamas' terrorists were not responsible for their atrocities against us. After all, they were poor, unfortunate, and powerless.

Yet I know full well, the facts tell a different story.

In 2005, Israel completed a unilateral disengagement from the Gaza Strip. Lilach and I publicly supported the withdrawal, demonstrating at weekly protests at road junctions near the border in the pouring rain and blazing sun. But two years later, Hamas violently seized control of the Gaza Strip, and from June 2007 onwards, it exercised absolute control over the territory.

From that year until October 7, 2023, the Hamas regime in Gaza enjoyed an enormous budget to the scale of $2.5–3 billion a year, meaning cumulatively, some $45–50 billion. The funding flowed from a range of sources: The Palestinian Authority, taxation on goods brought into the Gaza Strip, the United Nations, international donors, Iran, and Qatar. Israel lent a hand to

---

18 Gettleman, J., Schwartz, E. I., & Sella, A. (2023, December 28). *'Screams Without Words': How Hamas Weaponized Sexual Violence on Oct. 7. The New York Times*. https://www.nytimes.com/2023/12/28/world/middleeast/oct-7-attacks-hamas-israel-sexual-violence.html

all of this, operating under a paradigm that would later prove disastrous.

Hamas' leaders chose to use these vast funds not to improve the lives of the people of Gaza, but to advance their mission of global jihad and the annihilation of the State of Israel.

I became intimately familiar with that mission, seeing it firsthand from my long conversations with our captors, and from the fire-and-smoke posters on the walls of every house they held us in. But the nature of Hamas' mission should be perfectly plain to anyone who bothers to read what its jihadist ideologues have written across their media channels or to follow their public statements.

It is simply absurd to label them poor and powerless. Hamas' leaders managed gargantuan budgets and used them to employ around one hundred thousand people in the Gaza Strip, both in the Hamas-controlled health, education, and governing systems, and in its war machine. They built tunnel systems, both offensive and defensive, over 350 miles long with some 5,700 shafts, creating an underground network more extensive than even the New York City Subway.

They also managed to develop, acquire, and operate enormous quantities of weapons and missiles that only grew more advanced over the years. And they directed all these resources toward one goal: destroying Israel. Destroying us.

I recall a cartoon sketched by a friend from Be'eri during one of the many periods of tension with Hamas, after Israeli military intelligence uncovered some of their tunnels crossing into Israel. It depicts a terrorist peeking out of a concrete tunnel opening in the floor of the kibbutz dining hall near the buffet counters. He looks at the food trays, and the speech bubble from his mouth reads: "Ugh, schnitzel again? I'm sick of it." No one would dare draw such a cartoon nowadays. Reality erased any possibility of laughter.

Many countries have violent conflicts, but I know of none besides Iran (and its proxies: Hamas in Gaza, Hezbollah in Lebanon, and the Houthis in Yemen) that is actively plotting and pursuing the annihilation of another: Israel.

Iran's war is unique and draws on its jihadist agenda: First, to establish a state governed by sharia law on Israel's ruins, and then to realize its supreme goal of *jihad*, a holy struggle, a religious duty to pursue, through both violent and nonviolent means, a world order based on the absolute rule of Islam.

In the case of the attack against us from the Gaza Strip, the problem was much wider than the paid operatives of terror organizations. Those three thousand trained Hamas terrorists were not alone. Thousands of civilians also invaded Israeli communities and joined the murdering, kidnapping, and looting. I suspect that the young man with the crazed eyes, the one who violently cuffed my hands behind my back when we were dragged out of our safe room in Be'eri, was a civilian.

More than that, even deep into the war, when the scale of destruction in Gaza became plain to the civilians who were allowed to return home, few, if any, protested Hamas' October 7 atrocities. They protested the timing: It was too early, before Hamas was fully prepared, before Iran and its proxies' participation was assured. Their criticism was that the plan to destroy Israel failed.

***

Besides its campaign of psychological warfare, Hamas made use of another weapon in its October 7 attack. For the first time in history, a terror organization used the mass kidnapping of civilians to try to force geopolitical change. And with horrifying haste, nearly every country in the world normalized our kidnapping and captivity as legitimate parts of the Israeli–Palestinian conflict.

Even in Gaza, hearing the air force bombardments and the rocket fire toward Israel, I understood that Hamas carried out the assault knowing full well that the IDF would retaliate once it recovered from the shock. It knew in advance that the unprecedented scale of its attack would lead to an Israeli blow of exceptional force, which would inevitably harm the civilians behind whom Hamas terrorists hid in densely populated neighborhoods.

The harm to civilians in Gaza served Hamas' strategy as terrorist organization: It undermined Israel's political standing on the world stage. Hamas' leaders gladly sacrificed their own people's lives for this cause.

***

I try to shield myself from being overwhelmed by frustration and rage, so I avoid diving into the details of the investigations regarding the immense Israeli failure that led to the October 7 disaster. One thing is clear to me now, and it was just as clear to me during my time in captivity: Israel's political leadership and security agencies were all completely blind to the terrorists' thinking, specifically the centrality of jihad to their ideology, and they failed to correctly assess how deeply they were devoted to this cause.

On the other side, the terrorists and Palestinians in general suffer a different blindness. The Holocaust is deliberately absent from the school curriculum under the Palestinian Authority and in the Gaza Strip.

In one of my conversations with Son Muhammad, it dawns on me that he never learned about the Holocaust. No wonder: Hamas' leaders call the Holocaust "a lie invented by the Zionists," and consider support for Holocaust education a "war crime" and "a service to the Zionists."

Hamas exploited its control of Gaza's education system to impose its worldview, aiming to raise new generations of young radical Islamists, saturated with hatred for Israel and the West, ready to join its armed struggle. Their ignorance of the Holocaust led them into a fundamental misunderstanding of how tightly we—the Israelis, the Jews—cling to the State of Israel.

The attempted annihilation of the Jewish People when we were dispersed around the world, without a state of our own, is the bedrock of our devotion to an independent, democratic Jewish state. By misunderstanding this, the Palestinians misjudged the intensity of Israelis' reactions to their assault on October 7. They thought the scale of harm would push Jews to abandon Israel en masse; in practice, it only strengthened our connection with our country.

Primo Levi, who survived nearly a year in Auschwitz, describes in his books the figure of the Jew in the death camps as someone nobody sought to avenge, whose life nobody fought for, and whom nobody even regarded as an "asset" worth negotiating over. In the Shoah, the Jew was treated as raw refuse for annihilation; he had no backing, no state, and no voice.

I knew that our story was fundamentally different. For our captors, we were "assets": valuable bargaining chips, merchandise of geostrategic worth. Deep inside this carnage, this fact gave us a sliver of security. We understood that their interest was to keep us alive to blackmail Israel for concessions.

That is the historic difference between the Shoah and our own times: We, the Jews, have a state. The same state that on October 7 failed its most basic duty—protecting our lives—and immediately went to war for our liberation. This time, unlike in Levi's generation, we had the backing of a sovereign power. We heard fighting around us and knew we were not alone in the world, that a ferocious battle, both diplomatic and militaristic, was being fought for our sake. In time, we would also learn about the enormous public campaign for our release. We were physically cloistered, but our names and photographs were everywhere.

I am sure we are not going anywhere. We will stay here. In Israel. And as long as the Palestinians still aspire to destroy us, we will have to defend ourselves.

I mourn the missed opportunity of Israel's withdrawal from the Gaza Strip in 2005. From my experience as a humanitarian in Africa, I know that bringing major change to people's lives must begin with a pilot, one that proves, first to oneself and then to the world, that a model is workable, scalable, and sustainable.

When Lilach and I went out to demonstrate in support of the withdrawal, we believed with all our hearts that the people of Gaza would use their newfound freedom to build a better future; that they would develop the Gaza Strip, which could have been so beautiful, with its splendid beaches and fertile soil, and in doing so convince us, the Israelis, and the wider world, that we could all live here in peace.

But it was Hamas' takeover of Gaza's entire civilian infrastructure, and its abuse of the education system to steer the youth toward ideological jihadism, that led to tragedy and such immense suffering on both sides.

Today, with eyes wide open and a heavy heart, I realize we were all led to this grim situation because terrorist organizations in Gaza were fueled by massive streams of international funding.

Without that money, Hamas could not have seized control of the Gaza Strip and the minds of the people living there.

Flashbacks from captivity and conversations with Son Muhammad swirl through my mind. He taught me that Hamas is an organized, well-funded organization that pays monthly salaries to its operatives and assigns them tasks.

Murderers.

Kidnappers.

Captors.

In-house journalists.

Social-media influencers.

All the same.

All in the service of jihad, to annihilate us and place the world under the rule of Islam.

But who is masterminding this? Who is financing it all?

The thoughts gnaw away at me. I begin to read anything I can find about brainwashing. Over two years after the October 7 massacre, I come across a report by Itamar Eichner[19] on exactly this subject. The Institute for the Study of Global Antisemitism and Policy (ISGAP), a US research center, published a comprehensive report exposing the Muslim Brotherhood's "one-hundred-year plan" to conquer the West, with an alarming status update on the situation today, fifty years into that plan.

---

[19] Eichner, I. (2025, November 20). Report: How the Muslim Brotherhood seeks to undermine Western democracies. Ynetnews. https://www.ynetnews.com/article/r1r11x6jx11x

The full report[20], *The Muslim Brotherhood's Strategic Entryism into the United States: A Systemic Analysis*, is, according to Eichner, the first comprehensive strategic assessment of the Muslim Brotherhood's one-hundred-year plan at its midpoint. It is presented at an event hosted by the institute in Washington, DC, with members of Congress, high-ranking diplomats, policy experts, and leading scholars.

According to the report, the Muslim Brotherhood infiltrated the West as follows: Affiliated bodies gained access to government institutions, advised them on civil rights policies, influenced their education systems, and established media and digital networks as part of a strategy of "civilizational jihad," a long-term campaign intended to undermine Western democracies by exploiting freedom of religion and expression.

I read the report in astonishment. It describes how these bodies forged tactical alliances with progressive groups and minorities, while at the same time supporting terror organizations, including Hamas. They embedded themselves in core institutions in the United States and other Western societies in order to undermine and weaken their democracies, exploiting their freedoms and the tolerance of liberal societies.

Qatar, which supports the movement ideologically and financially, also exports its worldview through Al Jazeera and AJ+, a digital media outlet distributed mainly on YouTube, Facebook, Instagram, and X in English, Arabic, French and Spanish, as

---

[20] ISGAP. (2025, November 17). The Muslim Brotherhood's global project to undermine Western democracies. Institute for the Study of Global Antisemitism and Policy. https://isgap.org/wp-content/uploads/2025/11/MB-Project-Final-251117-01.pdf

outlined in the strategic analysis of digital influence[21]. Their content targets young people, especially millennials, many of whom consume content through social networks rather than traditional news channels. AJ+ has tens of millions of followers and billions of cumulative views, and its messages influence huge numbers of teenagers who have no idea that it is completely controlled by Qatar, which uses it for ideological influence.

Reading Eichner's report, I see a link to another piece, about a secret report commissioned by the French government and leaked to *Le Figaro* in May 2025[22]. To my surprise, I discovered that the author of the article is my friend, the journalist Tamar Sebok, with whom I wandered through Paris in September 2025 to find an outfit for Yuval and Anna-Lee's wedding. As we strolled through the city's magical alleyways, excited for the wedding, Tamar did not want to dampen my mood by telling me about her report; thus, it was only when I read Eichner's report that I learned of its existence

The report exposes the hidden mechanism through which Islamist extremists are expanding their influence in France through associations and online preachers, funded with Qatari and Saudi money, and it describes a global plan intended to instill the values of radical Islam in French society. The extent of the activity of Muslims of France, none other than the French branch of the Muslim Brotherhood, horrifies me. The report identifies at least 280 charities dealing with education, youth and children, culture, sports, and social and professional assistance

---

21 Zachor Legal Institute. (2023, March). The AJ+ strategy: Targeted influence and its impact on Western democracies. https://zachorlegal.org/wp-content/uploads/2023/03/AJ-Report-2023-WEB-VERSION.pdf

22 Sebok, T. (2024, May 21). Leaked Secret Report: How Qatar-Funded Muslim Brotherhood is Expanding Across France]Hebrew]. Ynet. https://www.ynet.co.il/news/article/r1n0s4owgx

as affiliated with radical Islam, operating dozens of centers of prayer and education across most regions of France.

The report raises concerns that France might experience something like what happened in Belgium, where Islamist parties have competed in local and national elections, with one even demanding the application of Sharia law. One of its conclusions is that France must fight the influence of the Muslim Brotherhood coming from within French society, and not only from foreign actors. At the end of Tamar's article, she notes that the names of the report's authors were not disclosed, apparently out of fear for their lives.

I finish reading, flustered, and wonder: Will France, which proudly bears the banner of "Liberty, Equality, Fraternity," not wake up to defend its values? And why was there an attempt to hide the report's findings from the public?

Have we gone blind again? Is the democratic, liberal world choosing to close its eyes to threats against its core beliefs and way of life?

This sinking feeling propels me on a deeper journey to unpack this phenomenon. I feel like I am walking down a long, dark corridor lined with heavy curtains that hide reality from me, and I pull back curtain after curtain, only to discover another layer behind each one threatening our daily lives. Just as I carefully pulled aside the curtains to examine the world around me in Gaza, despite the danger that our captors would notice and punish me, I do the same now.

My curiosity leads me to meet more and more people, and to glean more and more information and knowledge from them. Following one such meeting, I am shown data provided by American universities to the US Department of Education about donations from foreign entities from 2001 to 2025[23]. At many of these universities, protests supporting Hamas and the Palestinians erupted as early as October 9, 2023, merely two days after we were attacked and taken hostage.

I learn that four of the United States' leading universities reported that, during these years, they were lavishly funded by Qatar: Cornell University received about $2.3 billion from Qatar, seventy-five percent of its total foreign donations; Texas A&M received $990 million, ninety-five percent of its foreign donations; Georgetown received $970 million from Qatar, seventy-two percent of its foreign donations; and Virginia Commonwealth University received more than $330 million from Qatar, seventy-five percent of its foreign donations.

And when I read another report, *Shadows of Influence: Uncovering Hidden Foreign Funds to American Universities,* published at the end of 2024, I understand that in practice, all of these institutions have received far larger sums from Qatar but conceal some of the data from the authorities.[24]

I am flabbergasted. These colleges are producing the next generation of politicians, leaders, educators, journalists, and other figures of influence. And I have no doubt: Qatar's massive donations to American academic institutions have a clear purpose—to gain direct influence over university presidents and administrations, over the direction of research and development, over faculty, over the curricula, and over their students' minds and their future activism.

---

23 US Department of Education. (2025, February 28). Section 117 foreign gifts and contracts disclosure reports [Data set]. Federal Student Aid. https://studentaid.gov/data-center/school/foreign-gifts

24 Neetu Arnold, *Shadows of Influence: Uncovering Hidden Foreign Funds to American Universities* (National Association of Scholars, 2024).

On my first trip to the United States after my release from captivity, I am invited to a Shabbat meal at the home of one of the Jewish donors who jumped into action immediately after October 7 to support the campaign to bring the hostages home. As he tears the challah and passes it around to the guests, he remarks, "Our mistake was that we donated all these years to universities for buildings and labs—for hardware, not software."

The Muslim Brotherhood, spearheaded by Qatar, is heavily investing in the 'software' of influence. This encompasses not just digital platforms, but the use of sophisticated algorithms and cognitive framing designed to reshape Western consciousness and re-engineer social perceptions (ISGAP, 2025 - see ref. [16]) ; Zachor Legal Institute, 2023 - see ref. [17]). And in total defiance of the notion of academic independence and the sacred academic value of objectivity and intellectual independence, they have managed to inject their Islamist worldview into higher education institutions in the United States. Far smarter, in their view, than investing only in hardware. And far more dangerous to the free world.

And I know something I already understood in Gaza: The key to a better future in the Middle East is an effective global effort to stop funds reaching terrorist organizations and the mechanisms driving radical Islamization.

And the second most important thing for our region is fundamental reform of education in Gaza, the Palestinian Authority, and around the world, to gut them of radical Islamist and anti-Semitic content calling for regional and global jihad.

I am convinced that the terrible suffering of the people of Gaza could have been avoided if the effort to annihilate us in our homeland, which so many in the West echo with the chant "From the river to the sea!" perhaps not truly understanding what it means, were replaced with a global movement to invest in education for humanism, democracy, liberal values, and peaceful coexistence.

Only when that happens can we return to living side by side. Only then can we realize the shared vision of Women Wage Peace and Women of the Sun.

CHAPTER XVII
AN ENDING AND A BEGINNING

ON OCTOBER 13, 2025, ON the same day that all the surviving hostages are released, the President of the United States, Donald Trump, lands at Ben Gurion Airport. The timing, of course, is no coincidence. Trump drops into Israel for a few hours at a moment of national euphoria and is met with a hysterical welcome. From Prime Minister Netanyahu at the Knesset in Jerusalem, to more than one hundred thousand people crowding Hostages Square in Tel Aviv, he receives a standing ovation. At times, it feels like an entire country is worshiping him.

The spotlight on Trump is entirely justified. After many months in which Netanyahu and Hamas' leaders dug in their heels, and many received the impression that Trump had lost interest and turned to other matters, he decided to force a deal—classic Trump—in a manner that left the sides with no choice. His speech in the Knesset is long enough to smother Netanyahu with praise but also to describe how moved he is by the Israeli public's desire to see the hostages home and to declare that the use of military pressure to get them home is over.

Israel is thus compelled to withdraw from parts of the Gaza Strip without achieving all its goals, and Hamas is forced to agree to free all the hostages, the living and dead alike: The strongest card it holds. After two blood-soaked years, an agreement to end the war is finally signed. Near-total quiet suddenly settles over the fighting zones. The residents of the Israeli communities near the Gaza border, those who have already returned home, begin to breathe more easily.

But not freely yet. In a fairly absurd twist, Netanyahu is absent from the signing ceremony in Sharm el-Sheikh. Having landed in Egypt, Trump is flanked on stage by the leaders of Qatar and Turkey, two Sunni states that shelter Hamas and benefit greatly from the deal. What ended up pushing President Trump to press for an agreement was an Israeli attempt to assassinate senior Hamas figures with an airstrike in Doha, the capital of Qatar. The missiles missed the target and angered Trump, who had not approved the strike. Israel's failure therefore became an American lever of pressure.

Speaking in Jerusalem and Sharm el-Sheikh, Trump heralds the peace and prosperity around the corner. He speaks about disarming Hamas. Bringing more Arab states into the Abraham Accords. Ending the era of bloodshed.

But like many others, I know the difference between words and deeds, between a vision and the complexity of making it real. What will all this mean for the future of the Middle East? For regional alliances? For the security of Israelis living near the Gaza border, or anywhere else for that matter? Hamas has suffered a crushing blow, but even after two years of war, it has not been destroyed, certainly not as an idea nor as a terrorist organization that will break any deal it signs. At the time of writing, Hamas is still the dominant force in the Gaza Strip because it is still armed, and it acted despicably in delaying the return of the dead hostages buried in the Gaza Strip.

Meanwhile, the hostages who return to Israel alive reveal details of the horrific conditions they endured in captivity. Guy Gilboa-Dalal and Evyatar David were treated even more horribly after they were left without Tal and Omer Wenkert. Hamas released a video showing Evyatar frighteningly skinny, his bones protruding, digging his own grave deep in a tunnel. Guy was also deliberately starved, and the terrorists told him and Evyatar that they intended to turn them into walking skeletons. The two young men were separated and reunited only when they were released.

Elkana Bohbot, who was also shown in an increasingly desperate condition in Hamas' videos, was allowed to shower only once during his two years of captivity.

Avinatan Or, kidnapped from the Nova Festival, was held alone in tunnels for two years. For over a year, following an attempted escape, this six-foot-seven young man was locked in a cage only five feet eleven inches high.

Neither Ariel Cunio nor Rom Braslavski saw another hostage for two years.

Matan Angrest was beaten until he lost consciousness, electrocuted, and shackled to a gas canister for two weeks.

While blindfolded, Bar Kuperstein was repeatedly struck across the head with enough force to make his ears ring like cymbals. He was beaten on the soles of his feet and went for days without a single meal.

Eitan Horn lost 132 pounds.

This is just a sample of what hell truly looks like. A taste of the work of brainwashed terrorists, captive to their own sick, twisted faith.

Throughout the long and valiant struggle to free the hostages, I spoke to anyone who would listen and wrote for anyone who would read, hoping to convince the world that bringing the hostages home was the key to stopping the fighting, healing the Israeli people from the October 7 massacre, ending the suffering of the people of the Gaza Strip, and beginning its reconstruction.

Only now, two years too late, at the cost of so much blood and destruction, have I been proven right. The return of all the living hostages and the commitment to return the dead hostages made the end of the war possible. And yet, Hamas' continued sporadic fire at IDF forces and its deliberate procrastination when returning the dead hostages have made it clear that the conflict, broadly speaking, is not over and the road to the day after is still a minefield.

***

Meanwhile, I try to rebuild my life. In time, I join groups whose membership is determined by criteria nobody would choose to fulfill: a group for captivity survivors and another for widows and widowers. I follow the WhatsApp conversations in both groups and understand that the trauma we endured, which we still carry with us, is directly connected to the physical location where our loved ones were murdered or kidnapped, the place that cut our lives into two.

A before.

And an after.

Struck with the most colossal force on that day, our lives were thrown totally off track. And now here we are, metaphorically speaking, lying by the wayside while others around us go about their lives.

Many of us are still so furious, so mournful, so emotionally wounded that we struggle to imagine a future at all or work to build one.

Gradually, I begin to understand that the main barrier to recovery is the fear that we will never be able to settle into a home somewhere else, in a place that will not constantly evoke or preserve the memory of pain and trauma.

Once I identify the problem and the key to the solution, I get bitten by the entrepreneurial bug again and launch myself into a new mission. I marshal my connections and powers of persuasion to rope others into the initiative, and together we establish a new nonprofit: ReHome. We recruit top professionals—real estate developers, lawyers, financiers, mortgage brokers—anyone who can help give the victims guidance through the complicated process of locating and buying a new home on the road to rebuilding their future. To recovery.

I am deeply moved by the desire of so many people to contribute and support, and this activity gives me a significant amount of strength. Instead of turning inward and focusing on my own personal tragedy, I begin to pivot to helping others, toward action and volunteering.

***

As the second anniversary of October 7 approaches, the Israeli Embassy in Ethiopia invites me to participate in a memorial ceremony in Addis Ababa. The embassy staff, fully aware of our longstanding connection at Fair Planet with this country, ask me to speak at the event, to be attended by senior representatives of the Ethiopian government, foreign ambassadors, members of the Jewish community, and the media. I oblige, despite my fear of confronting the inconceivable dissonance between the depth of the disaster that still rattles me in my current life and the height of my achievement in my previous one.

Naturally, I ask Fair Planet Chairman Amnon Tamir, with whom I made my first-ever trip to Africa and began my journey at Fair Planet, to join me. I also ask the embassy to invite the two dear people who anchored our work in Ethiopia. The first is Amerga Menji, a senior agricultural expert who runs a nursery producing top-tier avocado saplings in Butajira, where we conducted our first vegetable variety trial in the fall of 2012 and with whom we led our project in western Ethiopia. The second is Professor Kebede Woldetsadik, vice president of Haramaya University, who has led our work in the eastern Ethiopia.

Indeed, my fears about the emotional complexity of the visit prove warranted. I feel like I am on a roller coaster, flitting between interviews about the disaster of October 7 and conversations with Amerga and Kebede, who report enthusiastically on the project's dazzling success in Ethiopia.

Amerga tells us that the shift to high-quality seeds and more efficient cultivation methods has yielded a dramatic rise in income for many farmers in the region. After recounting the project's wider impact, he describes the successes of Nuri, Taji, Jembero, and other farmers we trained early on. Nuri, whom we are especially fond of, even planted a row of avocado trees and his family enjoys additional income from selling their cuttings. We are sad to hear from Amerga that Nuri was ill and passed away, but his eldest son has taken over.

Kebede, for his part, reminds us of his original vision. When we met, the most profitable crop in eastern Ethiopia was khat. Knowing that chewing khat may stimulate and lift the mood but leads to hours of idleness, lethargy, and poverty, Kebede hoped that cultivating higher-quality vegetables would give farmers in the region a better economic alternative. And now, he reports, our project has made his vision a reality: Many farmers in eastern Ethiopia have converted their fields to supply their local communities with fresh vegetables, earning them more money than they did from growing khat. The supply of those intoxicating leaves dwindles, along with their harmful influence on consumers.

In the evening, the embassy staff invites us all to a social gathering. When Amnon and I enter the large room, we spot Segev Marom. One of Fair Planet's most devoted volunteers, he fell in love with Ethiopia during the volunteering period and was hired to work at Joytech's seedling nursery not far from Addis Ababa.

When we began working in Ethiopia, we contacted Joytech's owners, who at the time were focusing on growing and exporting herbs to Europe. We asked them to produce small quantities of saplings for us for our variety trials, and although the request fell outside the business production line they had built, they immediately understood the importance and obliged.

Segev updates us excitedly that today, the nursery is the largest vegetable seedling supplier in Ethiopia, selling more than seventy million seedlings a year to local farmers, out of a growing annual market of more than two hundred million seedlings. With a glimmer in his eyes, he notes that a range of international seed companies have since entered Ethiopia and are competing with each other on seed prices and the quality of their service to farmers.

Within all my emotional turbulence, I understand that Fair Planet's presence in Ethiopia is no longer needed. The bridge we built between the world's best seeds and Ethiopia's famers is already functional and growing. Farmers have adopted the know-how, grasping the immense economic value of using high-quality seeds. Seed companies have understood that small farmers are lucrative customers. As a result, they have expanded their activity in Ethiopia, hiring their own instructors, expanding the influence of our project through its own expanding ripples, exactly as we had hoped when we set out.

Satisfied by this success in Ethiopia, I am even more convinced now that the principle on which our project was founded can succeed and propel farmers forward elsewhere in Africa, as we begin to demonstrate in Tanzania and Rwanda. For that, we need to raise financial resources and expand our professional partnerships. It's an immense challenge that, in my current state, I cannot devote all my energy to, but that is so important that I would be glad if someone else could be found to make it a reality.

The wheels of the plane taking off from Addis Ababa descend before we land back in Israel, bringing me back to the reality of my new life.

***

One day, quite a long time after I return from captivity, I receive a text message from my brother Aviv that some of our sister Lilach's clothes were saved from the inferno the terrorists started in her home. They were washed three times to remove the smell of smoke, and he stored them at home all this time.

Would I want them? After some hesitation and deliberation, I text him *Yes, please.*

Aviv brings the clothes to my temporary home in Herzliya, folded in bags, and places them in the entryway. Days pass, and every time I walk by the bags, I look at them and cannot bring myself to open them. I am afraid of touching the fabric that were once so intimately pressed against Lilach's body. Weeks pass, and the bags are still closed, lying in the same place. I cannot ignore them, and I cannot touch them.

Three months later, a good friend comes to visit. I ask her if she might help me, be with me, and help me open what I dare not open alone. We drag the bulging bags upstairs to my bedroom, sit on the bed, open bag after bag, and in fear, take out each item: cotton shirts with delicate, colorful prints; floral tunics; a white shirt with a large embroidered flower above the chest. Cheerful clothes that perfectly embody my sister's spirit: optimistic, cheerful, beloved. We touch each item gently, fold them carefully, and stack them all in a neat pile in my closet.

Since then, every time I open the closet, I see them and remember her. But even though our sizes are similar, and I love her clothes, I cannot wear them. I feel that if I do, I will see her looking back at me in the mirror. I will see Lilach, my little sister, who is gone. I cannot.

***

I feel the passage of time hardening the shell I inhabit. Deep in my heart is a terrible grief for everyone whose life was cut short, for my own life without them.

I struggle with the difficulties of being alone, learning to plan my day in order to not break down under the weight of loneliness in the afternoon, when so many people finish work and go back home to their spouses and families, to the most pleasant hours of their day. I fill up the empty days, like a quilt, with meetings with a good friend here or there, trying to find the right balance between finding relief and being careful not to overburden others.

Ahead of every weekend, I must plan where I will be. Will the children and grandchildren come to me for Shabbat, which is what I desire most, or will I make other plans and go to them, to friends, or to some more distant relatives?

In my past life, with Avshal at my side, everything flowed so naturally. Now every step must be calculated, lest loneliness come knocking with a force that crushes my soul.

***

Today—November 2, 2025—for the umpteenth time, I reread the final sentences of Stefan Zweig's *The World of Yesterday*:

> "But in the last resort, every shadow is also the child of light, and only those who have known the light and the dark, have seen war and peace, rise and fall, have truly lived their lives."

But this time, I do not connect to his words. War is unnecessary. The suffering it causes everyone has no purpose. I do not feel that my horrific ordeal means that now, only now, have I truly lived.

I must muster the strength to blaze my own path from now on, without my Avshal, without Lilach or Tari. I carry with me the memory of the 102 people of Kibbutz Be'eri murdered on October 7, the nearly 1,200 victims of that horrific massacre, and the heavy toll of the soldiers who fell in the ensuing war, fighting with such bravery to protect our homeland.

With renewed strength and a most profound recognition of the need to strive for a better world, I report for duty before the future.

ACKNOWLEDGMENTS

THIS BOOK WAS BORN THANKS to those who stood by me in moments of anxiety and hope. Together, we have traveled a path of family survival spanning three generations. Without your presence, support, and faith in me, I would not have been able to write this book.

First and foremost, I wish to thank my partners in fate: my daughter Adi Shoham, who shared this journey with me, both in real life and in committing it to text; my son-in-law Tal Shoham, who returned to us having suffered the worst human cruelty to share his testimony; my grandchildren Naveh and Yula, who experienced things no child should ever have to endure and whose inner strength inspires us all; and my sister-in-law Sharon Avigdori and her daughter Noam, who were swept into the inferno with us and from which we returned, together.

Thank you to my son Yuval Haran, who rallied tens of thousands to demand our release; to his wife, Anna-Lee Milstein, who joined his campaign with vigor; to my daughter Shaked Haran-Forer, who fought across the world for our return and the freedom of all the hostages; to her husband, Daniel, who supported her and provided a steady anchor; and to their children, Nahar Shalom and Sinai Moshe, who appeared in my dreams in

Gaza, when my longing for them filled me with strength; and to my two granddaughters born after my return, Ora Bra Rina and Noga, who brought light and joy into our lives.

A special thank you to my brother Aviv Havron, who fought for us with every tool at his disposal and edited this book with love and creativity, helping me weave thousands of fragments of a shattering experience into a complete picture.

Thank you to Gila Havron, Aviv's wife, and to their children Shira, Omer, and Ella, who campaigned for our release on multiple fronts.

Thank you as well to my brother David Havron, his wife Ayala, and their children Naomi, Rafi, and Boaz; to Yotam and Nadav Kipnis, the sons of my sister Lilach, of blessed memory, and my brother-in-law Evyatar, of blessed memory, who were taken from us on that cursed day; and to all the members of my extended family, who fought for us, embraced us, and created a protective network around us.

Thank you to Daniel Donne, who encouraged me to write and opened the gates of the literary world to me.

Thank you to my agents at The Blair Partnership, Neil Blair and Rory Scarfe, for their unwavering faith in the importance of this book and for their guidance from the very beginning. And to Sarah Passick at Park, Fine & Brower for her enthusiastic support.

Thank you to Anat Ben Ze'ev Shinkman, Yael Ne'eman, and Re'ut Borovik Baruch, who commented on and refined the manuscript with wisdom and care.

Thank you to the team at Yedioth Books, led by CEO Dov Eichenwald, who took on the publishing of this book as a mission; and to Ruti Ben Ari, who attended to every detail with professionalism and sensitivity. My deepest thanks go to Eylon

Levy for his superb English translation; to Ashlyn Inman for her expert editorial eye and for ensuring the precision of every page and reference; and to David Bernstein at Wicked Son for opening the door and helping me bring this story to the English-speaking world.

Thank you to Tomer Amir, who dedicated his enormous heart and remarkable abilities to overcome every challenge; to Ayelet Hirshman for her enriching literary advice; to Michal Arlozorov, who wisely helped me navigate all matters relating to the rights over the book; to Amnon Tamir, who was able to sift through and distill mountains of data and to his wife, Ariane, who led the fight to free us in France.

Thank you to all my devoted friends who were there in my darkest hours and knew when to ask questions and when simply to be present.

And finally, thanks to you, the readers. By coming to know this story, you imbue it with more power and expand its reach beyond its pages and into reality itself.

ABOUT THE AUTHOR

Shoshan Haran with her daughter Adi, son-in-law Tal and grandchildren Naveh and Yahel after their release (Photo by Avigail Uzi).

DR. SHOSHAN HARAN IS A humanitarian leader and the founder of FairPlanet, a nonprofit dedicated to providing smallholder farmers in developing countries with food and economic security. Her life's work was met with unimaginable tragedy on October 7, 2023, when she was kidnapped from Kibbutz Be'eri and held hostage in Gaza for fifty days alongside her daughter and grandchildren. Despite the murder of her husband and close family members during the attack, Dr. Haran has emerged as a powerful global witness. In her book, *Mission in Captivity*, she shares a profound story of survival and resilience that transcends politics. By testifying before international bodies and sharing her journey with audiences worldwide, she has become a vital voice for humanity, alerting the world to the universal threat of terrorism and the enduring power of hope.